igloo

Published in 2011
by Igloo Books Ltd
Cottage Farm
Sywell
NN6 OBJ

www.igloo-books.com

L006 1111

10 9 8 7 6 5 4 3 2 1

ISBN: 978-0-85780-241-5

Printed and manufactured in China

101

101 PLACES

to SEE BEFORE YOU die

igloo

CONTENTS

EVENTS

MONUMENTS

CULTURE

WONDERS

HISTORIC

ADVENTURE

PORTOBELLO MARKET
LONDON, UK

ne of the most famous street markets in the world! Portobello Market runs through London's fashionable Notting Hill. The area that is now in the heart of London was originally a farm, named Portobello in memory of Admiral Vernon who captured the Caribbean town of Puerto Bello in 1739.

The market is situated on Portobello Road, with stalls running the length of the street for almost two miles. You can buy just about anything here, from vintage fashion to groceries, but the market is truly famous for its antiques stalls. Around 2,000 antiques dealers operate from here, some from upmarket shops, others sharing small temporary pitches.

Lose yourself for hours browsing the stalls, stopping every now and then for a welcome rest and refreshments. You're spoilt for choice when it comes to food. As well as traditional market fare, there are plenty of eateries offering everything from pizzas to authentic Thai cuisine.

The market opened in 1870 when workers spent their Saturdays browsing stalls, relaxing after a hard week in factories. It became so popular that traders persuaded the council to let them open six days a week from 1927. Nowadays, the market is open from Monday to Saturday.

The market is open from 6 am. It's advisable to get there early to avoid heavy crowds and make sure you get a look-in at the best stuff first.

spoilt

FOR

CHOICE

ORGANISED food fight FESTIVAL

LA TOMATINA FESTIVAL
VALENCIA, SPAIN

Like tomatoes? Don't mind getting a bit messy? Or a lot messy? Then La Tomatina is for you! You know your mum told you never to play with your food? Well forget it. La Tomatina actively encourages you to muck about with this squashy red food staple. It's an organised food fight festival that takes place on the last Wednesday in August.

Join the thousands of others who head over to the town of Valencia in Spain for what has become known as the World's Biggest Food Fight, which makes spilling the ketchup look like child's play.

To take part, it helps if you like getting messy and don't mind crowds, as up to 40,000 people have been known to join in. Get there early on the day as trucks start to bring in the tomatoes at around 10 am. Technically La Tomatina doesn't start until one person has climbed a greasy pole and collected a ham from the top, but in reality smashed, mashed, tomato fun starts before that happens.

Water cannons are fired to start the fight and it's everyone for themselves. Wear goggles and old clothes! All tomatoes must be squashed before throwing for safety reasons. After exactly one hour, the event is over and the big clean up starts with fire engines hosing down the streets, though not the people. Many of those taking part end up washing off the red gunk in the River Bunol.

If you do fancy getting soaked in tomato squish, go for it. But remember Bunol is a tiny town. Most revellers choose to stay in nearby Valencia and travel in for the event.

Happy splatting!

CHRISTMAS MARKET
NUREMBERG, GERMANY

his magical shopping experience in the bewitching old quarter of Nuremberg will make even the grumpiest Scrooge feel festive. The two million people who visit this market every year can't be wrong!

The famous Christkindlesmarkt on Haupmarkt Square opens every year on the Friday before Advent Sunday (the fourth Sunday before Christmas). At 5.30pm, the Christmas Angel recites a solemn prologue from the Church of our Lady and the market is officially up and running. It closes for business on Christmas Eve.

Here you can soak up the medieval charm of the quaint German streets and be swept away with the spicy aromas of gingerbread and warming glühwein, or feel those stomachs rumble as you smell the wafting sizzles of local bratwurst (sausage) cooking in the chill night air.

So, what to buy? Food, inevitably! Start with traditional wares like fruit loaves and Nuremberg's own spicy gingerbread. Pop a few Nuremberg Plum People in your shopping bag, as stowaways for the journey home. These are cute little figurines made from prunes. You will also come across some of the most delightful festive gifts including cribs, tree ornaments and traditional children's toys. Close by is the Nuremberg Kinderweihnacht, a market especially geared towards children with a captivating carousel, old-fashioned Ferris wheel and a steam train.

soak up

the MEDIEVAL CHARM

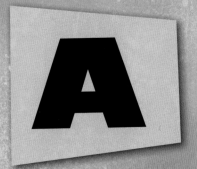

weekend OF A LIFETIME

NOTTING HILL

LONDON, UK

Close your eyes and let yourself be swept away by the smells and sounds of the Caribbean. Only when you open them again do you realise that you couldn't be further away from the dusty towns and sandy beaches of sea-fringed islands!

You're at the Notting Hill Carnival, the largest festival of its kind in the whole of Europe. Dive right in and immerse yourself in the fun and friendliness that have become bywords for this annual event.

Held every August Bank Holiday Sunday and Monday, this event takes in miles and miles of West London and attracts around a million revellers every year. It couldn't go ahead without the dedication and hard work of the 40,000 volunteers who spend 11 months of the year getting ready for the weekend of a lifetime.

It originated back in 1964 as a way for people from Afro-Caribbean communities to get together. Its roots lie in the Caribbean carnival tradition of celebrating freedom and the abolition of the slave trade, particularly in Trinidad.

Today, Notting Hill Carnival is a true feast for the eyes (and taste buds) and houses an array of fabulous music and classic Caribbean favourites including: jerk chicken, rice and delicious rum punch.

Get there early! On both days, steel band action gets going around 10 am, with the eye-popping parades due to finish their lengthy processions in the early evening.

GLASTONBURY FESTIVAL

SOMERSET, UK

If you only go to one music festival in your life, then this has to be it. It's the largest greenfield music and performing arts festival in the world – and many other successful events have followed its format. Brave the mud and long queues to live for the moment in music heaven.

'Glasto' as it is known, may have a reputation for being rainy, muddy and generally uncomfortable from a camping point of view, but ask anyone who's been and they'll tell you the lack of creature comforts more than makes up for the fantastic array of bands and performers who step on to the many stages.

The very first festival was held in September 1970, the day after Jimi Hendrix died. It lasted two days and Marc Bolan and Al Stewart were among the acts who wowed the 1,500 crowd. Over 40 years on, 'Glasto' is held most years and attracts over 135,000 visitors over the weekend.

There will be no event in 2012 as it's a fallow year for the farm. This gives organisers plenty of time to plan the June 2013 event which now attracts a huge range of musical artists who would previously never have been expected to appear. Who would have thought that Lady Gaga, Beyoncé, Foo Fighters and U2 would play at an event which once was the home of rockers like Peter Gabriel and David Bowie?

MARDI GRAS
RIO DE JANEIRO, BRAZIL

Do you want to party? Then save up and head to the carnival capital of the world, Rio de Janeiro, home to the best carnival of all, the Mardi Gras Carnival in Brazil's ritziest city. It's a mass of color, music and outrageous costume, a day of feasting and fun wrapped up in religious traditions. Mardi Gras (literally meaning Fat Tuesday) is the equivalent of Shrove Tuesday.

The Portuguese brought the idea of carnivals to Brazil over 150 years ago. They started as 'riots' before authorities allowed them to take place. Gradually costumes got wilder and music louder until we have the Mardi Gras of today, with elaborate clothes, fantastical performances and wondrous processions through the streets.

People from the poorest neighbourhoods save all year round to join in the festivities, spending hours on costumes and practising routines. Drag Queens turn out as some of the most glamorous ladies around and many people cross dress for kicks.

Though it's called Mardi Gras, the action starts the Friday before with the crowning of the carnival king, who receives the keys to the city. From then on in it's party, party, party, with events and processions throughout the city. Sunday and Monday are THE parade days that gave Rio its name as carnival capital of the world.

There are also balls galore to go to during the festivities. Costumes are optional at these, but if you really want to be part of it, spend plenty of time planning your sparkling outfit. Mardi Gras carnival really is one of life's massive memorable experiences – and glamming yourself up, whether in costume or ball gown, makes it even better!

FILM FESTIVAL

CANNES, FRANCE

ollywood comes to the Med, big time! If you love movies and love the glamour of the acting world, then head to Cannes, home to the rich and gorgeous, the place to moor your yacht and be seen. Like many things, the Cannes Film Festival was created to rival another event. Frenchman Jean Zay wanted a film festival to rival one that was already happening in Venice.

Planning started in the 1930s but the first Cannes film Festival didn't happen until 1946 after the Second World War was over. The first few festivals were more of a social event, but when star actors began appearing on the red carpet, the world pricked up its ears and took notice. Suddenly, Cannes became the place to be for anyone in the film industry.

The Cannes Film Festival is held every May. A lot of the events are by invitation only, but there are stacks of opportunities to soak up the atmosphere, go star-spotting and generally immerse yourself in that unique combination of Hollywood glitz and French chic. There are, however, quite a few screenings that the public can attend, but you need to be quick. The old first come, first served adage was never more true than here.

You could bump into an actor, director, screenwriter anywhere. Walk La Croisette in search of a star or starlet and you never know, Brad Pitt might be wandering down the street or Daniel Craig could be just around the corner. The biggest attraction for anyone with a love of movies, and the whole film industry though, is the whole feel of the place!

soak  the

MORE THAN

1,000

hours **of**

MUSIC

JAZZ FESTIVAL
MONTREUX, SWITZERLAND

If you thought Switzerland was all skiing and fancy chocolate, then think again! It's home to one of the snazziest jazz events on the worldwide calendar. The Montreux Jazz Festival was founded by Claude Nobs in 1967 and over the years has attracted many of music's greats, including Ray Charles, David Bowie and Prince.

The Festival runs for two weeks in July, with gigs at 12 venues, many of which are free. During the fortnight, over 1000 musicians will play more than 1000 hours of music, watched by 230,000 visitors! There are so many different types of events that it's good to plan in advance.

Montreux itself is a gorgeous town in a fab location. It nestles at the foot of the Alps on Lake Geneva and locals refer to it as the Swiss Riviera. There is a vast range of accommodation, from high class hotels to more modest places to stay. Like many festivals, Montreux is one where you can soak up the atmosphere just by being there.

It's child-friendly too, so long as your kids are over the age of six. Youngsters under the age of 16 have to be accompanied by an adult if they are going to watch a gig. Head down to the Festival's quays for food choices to satisfy even the fussiest eater. With stalls selling everything from Swiss specialities, to ice cream, fast food and more eclectic fare, there is plenty of choice!

Organisation is impeccable, right down to public transport services. There is even a pyjama bus running into the early hours of the morning to get jazz revellers safely back to their hotels at the end of an ear-splitting evening!

FASHION WEEK
WORLDWIDE

If you love clothes, adore fashion and would love a chance to soak up the world of haute couture, then head to one of the four fashion capitals of the world during Fashion Week: New York, London, Milan or Paris. Each city holds a Fashion Week twice a year, with New York kicking off and the other cities following.

The second being London, then Milan, with Paris having the grand finale. The very first Fashion Week happened in New York in 1943, in an attempt by the Americans to encourage people to take an interest in US designers instead of the French fashion houses. Until then, US fashion journalists frowned upon locally-created clothes, believing that Paris was the be-all of the right clothes to wear.

Attendance at most collection launches is strictly by invitation only, but if you're desperate to see the latest looks and if you know your designers, make sure you're in one of the four great fashion cities during their Fashion Week.

You'll be able to spot some of the most influential people in fashion as they arrive for the shows, wow at the gorgeousness of giraffe-like models as they arrive, and then read all about it in the press the next day. Combine your trip as part of a sightseeing holiday and chances are, you won't be disappointed!

gorgeous LITTLE getaway

GRAND PRIX

MONACO

The main event in the Formula 1 calendar! If you only see one car race in your life, make sure it's this one, a second-by-second thrill run. Unlike the other Formula 1 races, the Monaco Grand Prix doesn't take place on a purpose-built track. Instead, every May, the winding streets of this tiny principality become a white-knuckle racetrack for a once-a-year-thrill.

Monaco is already one of the coolest places of the planet to visit. It's a tiny principality ruled by Prince Albert, the son of Prince Rainier and his film star wife Grace Kelly. A place of high-class homes and luxury lifestyles, it is characterised by its harbour crammed with million dollar yachts. A tax-free haven, it attracts some of the richest celebrities in the world, who choose to live in this gorgeous little bolthole on the Med.

This Grand Prix is unique in that it has been run on the same course with few changes, since 1929. Known as the Circuit de Monaco, it offers a nailbiting view with twists, turns and sharp bends that call for seriously hot driving skills. There is little room for driver error at Monaco – and if it wasn't already such an established race, there is no way that a circuit like this would be added to the Formula 1 schedule in today's climate of health and safety.

If you want to be part of what is considered to be the jewel in the Formula 1 crown then you need plenty of cash and forward planning. It's not one to do on a shoestring and with demand high and accommodation limited, it's one of those once-in-a- lifetime experiences where you just have to grin, pay up and soak up the luxury atmosphere at the place where all the beautiful people just love to be seen!

OKTOBERFEST
MUNICH, GERMANY

ne for the beer aficionado! This massive event takes place every year in the southern German city of Munich. And when we say massive, we mean massive, from the size of the beer glasses to the numbers of people who attend.

Every year Oktoberfest (which despite the name, starts in September) attracts a staggering six million visitors. But there's more to Oktoberfest than just beer. It's two weeks of lively entertainment, from costume parades to fairground rides and brass band performances.

The event kicks off on a Saturday when the reigning Mayor of Munich officially 'taps' open the first beer barrel. Across the city there are 14 'tents', but if you think that means grotty old canvas, think again. Each of the 14 tents has its own unique personality.

Among the choices for revellers are Schiebl's Kaffeehaferl, which specialises in strudels, rich cakes and a vast selection of coffee, Käfer's Wies'n-Schänke, a tent with gourmet food and a big haunt of celebrity visitors. Seriously popular is the Hacker tent, known locally as Bavarian heaven. And if you're worried about space inside, then don't fret. The Hacker tent alone seats a staggering 9,300 people!

Even without the amber glow of beer drinking, Munich is a lovely city full of friendly locals. Nestling in the heart of Bavaria, it's one of Germany's prettiest places, so make the time to do a spot of sight-seeing while you're there.

not FOR the PRUDISH

MARDI GRAS

NEW ORLEANS, USA

Set off for the steamy southern city of New Orleans to experience Mardi Gras, American style. An explosive mix of cultures, colours, sights and sounds all nestled in the heart of Louisiana, will stay with you forever. Like Rio, the event is the same as Shrove Tuesday and starts the weekend before.

Mardi Gras has long been a part of New Orleans life. The city sprang up in the early 1700s and by the 1740s, balls were held to celebrate the event with carnivals taking hold in the 1780s. By 1870 it became even more dramatic, when a group of businessmen introduced a King of Carnival, known as Rex and brought in the official colours of purple, green and gold, along with a Mardi Gras flag and song.

So what can you expect? Watch out for Mardi Gras Throws. This dates back to the throwing of trinkets to the crowds in the 1870s and now doubloon coins are tossed into the crowds during the Bacchus parade. They are brightly coloured and catching one is considered good luck. Other popular Throws include cups, soft toys and strings of beads!

Mardi Gras is not for the prudish. You'll see Drag Queens, cross dressers and women revellers who will bare their breasts for the chance of a coveted string of beads. There are also grand balls you can book to attend, where dressing up may not be mandatory but you'll certainly feel out of place if you pitch up in jeans and sneakers.

Book ahead and expect to stay a while. Most hotels will insist on four or five night stays. Use public transport to the French Quarter, where most of the action and the parades take place.

DIWALI FESTIVAL
INDIA

Diwali is the biggest celebration on the Hindu calendar, and as India is home to more Hindus than anywhere else in the world, it's a great place to be part of this mesmerising spectacle. Jains and Sikhs also celebrate this uplifting festival.

This festival of truth and light (also known as Deepavali) is celebrated on a nationwide scale in India on Amavasya, the 15th day of the dark fortnight of the Hindu month of Aswin. The actual date varies each year but is usually in October or November.

In India, it's even more bewitching as whole neighbourhoods throw themselves into the celebrations. Diwali honours the Goddess Lakshmi, the goddess of wealth. And that means lots of lights, fire crackers, sweets and masses of opportunities to go shopping! People light small clay lamps filled with oil to signify the triumph of good over evil.

Celebrations tend to last five days, with the third day being the most important. People clean their homes and decorate them with colourful lights, setting off fire crackers to express their happiness. Everyone wears new clothes and big family gatherings happen everywhere.

If you're planning a trip to India, finding yourself there during Diwali is likely to be the highlight of your trip, with fantastic food, terrific light displays and plenty of wonderful shopping bargains to be had!

festival of

truth

AND

LIGHT

ancient

rituals

and

TRADITIONS

CHINESE NEW YEAR
HONG KONG, CHINA

Chinese New Year is a holiday celebration that is unique in the world calendar, a mesmerising mix of ancient rituals and traditions wrapped up with a modern twist. Across the globe, Chinese communities celebrate in style but the ultimate place to welcome the Chinese New Year, is in the tightly packed melting pot that is Hong Kong.

The actual date of Chinese New Year varies, but it mainly falls some time in late January or early February and it really is a wonderful assault on the senses, from fragrant flower markets to the sky filled with the fizz of fireworks, from dramatic parades to magnificent banquets, Hong Kong has it all.

Chinese New Year follows a 12-year cycle and depending what animal is represented, the celebrations are planned accordingly! The centrepiece of celebrations is the Cathay Pacific International Chinese New Year Night Parade, a massive spectacle featuring dressed floats, dragon and lion dancers, all interspersed with marching bands and clowns of all shapes and sizes.

The Chinese see the New Year as a time to give thanks for the past 12 months. Step out of the noise and bustle and join the crowds as they make a pilgrimage to Sik Sik Yuen Wong Tai Sin Temple. Here you can make a wish and hope that it will come true. It's a glorious piece of architecture that offers an oasis of calm. While you're there, it's hard to believe that the bustle of Hong Kong streets is only minutes away.

And don't miss the Symphony of Lights, an eye-popping multi-media show. Every night buildings on both sides of Hong Kong's Victoria harbour are illuminated with a phenomenal array of lights and lasers.

VENICE CARNIVAL
VENICE, ITALY

The floating city of Venice is a must-see destination in its own right, but visit when it's carnival time and you'll think you've died and gone to heaven! Carnivals have been huge in the Italian city since 1296 when the Senate of the Republic made Shrove Tuesday, the day before the start of Lent, a public holiday. But it has more than just religious significance. Locals celebrate it as the passage out of grim dark winter into fresh green spring. It's a time when anything can happen, when poor and rich can mingle.

Masked events are hugely popular at the Venice Carnival, the idea being that poor people can mix with the rich. Nowadays, the Carnival atmosphere is evident for a whole two weeks before the start of Lent. Venice may be known as La Serenissima, meaning the serene place, but Carnival time is when all the serenity is sidelined for flamboyant elegance. If you plan to go, make sure you plan to dress up! Costumes can be hired in Venice, or be daring and take your own.

Imagine drifting along its romantic canals in a gondola with your face concealed behind a mysterious mask; for a few short days you can be anyone you want to be. Make sure you're around for the last Saturday of the event when the Grand Canal comes to life with a torchlit procession of gondolas filled with revellers in the most exotic and romantic costumes. If you fall in love with a place only once, make it Venice at Carnival time.

watch

CREATIVE

BRAINS

FRINGE FESTIVAL

EDINBURGH, UK

Head to the Scottish capital in August for the world's largest arts festival, crammed with stacks of experimental drama, music and comedy. To get the best out of the event, you need a spreadsheet to keep track of all the performances taking place in a range of venues across the city.

The event started in 1947 as a reaction to the first Edinburgh International Festival. A group of theatre companies turned up uninvited and put on their own shows around the 'fringe' of big events. In the past few years, The Fringe, as it is now known, has become a breeding ground for new and innovative talent and a place where existing top performers can trial new material.

Nowadays, there are over 2,000 shows in more than 250 venues, from back rooms in bars, to cafes, basements and even warehouses. If you like your entertainment safe and mainstream then the Fringe is probably not for you. But if you're happy to watch creative brains pull out the very latest concepts in front of you, then go for it.

The essence of The Fringe is friendly camaraderie. During the event, the city has a genuine laid-back easy-going feel. It's a great way to see daring new acts and watch their progress as they hit the big time.

Book your accommodation early and keep a check on the show timetables when they are released. Like many events, some shows book up quick, while at others you can pay an entry free at the door. Don't forget to try some classic Scottish cuisine while you're there and indulge in many local delights, including homemade shortbread and haggis.

ARTS FESTIVAL
MELBOURNE, AUSTRALIA

If you didn't think that Australia was the home of arts festivals, think again! Across the country there are festivals galore, with the Melbourne International Arts Festival taking place every October.

It's seen as the flagship festival in Australia, attracting a huge number of artists from within the country as well as overseas. Every October, Melbourne is transformed into a hive of artistic activity for two weeks of scintillating entertainment to suit all comers.

The melting pot of shows is hard to quantify, there is everything from opera and serious theatre to the very latest in experimental bands, singers and performers. Throw in a stack of visual art exhibitions, from sculpture to paintings, along with opportunities to discuss ideas with performers and you have a real roller coaster of a festival.

It's a great time of year to be in Melbourne too as the antipodean winter gives way to a balmy spring and perfect temperatures for travelling across the city for performances. People of over 140 nationalities live here year round so there's never a chance that you'll feel like an outsider.

The city is home to lots of award-winning restaurants, catering for even the fussiest of eaters. For visitors on a tight budget, there are plenty of opportunities to find cheap and filling delights.

melting

pot

of

shows

THANKSGIVING PARADE
NEW YORK, USA

They say that Thanksgiving is bigger in the US than Christmas. And if you head to New York for the celebrations you won't be a bit surprised. Make sure you plan ahead for a truly memorable experience.

The Thanksgiving Holiday falls on the third Thursday of November and commemorates the first successful harvest of the Pilgrim Fathers who landed at Plymouth Sound. Nowadays the Thanksgiving parades that take place across the country are a huge celebration of thanks for everything people have in modern day America.

New York's parade is one of the biggest and brashest of them all. It began in 1924 by workers at Macy's department store and the first parade featured animals from New York zoo! Nowadays, three million people line the streets of Manhattan for the two-mile parade route so there's plenty of competition for space.

Almost as much fun as the parade itself, is the Balloon Set Up, held the day before Thanksgiving. Grab yourself a warming hot chocolate and head for the American Museum of Natural History and watch the balloons being blown up. The Parade starts at 9am on Thanksgiving Day, so you'll need to have picked your spot by 7am or risk a poor view. Best places to pitch are on 7th Avenue between Times Square and Macy's on 34th Street.

No trip to New York during Thanksgiving would be complete without trying a full Thanksgiving dinner. Hundreds of restaurants offer mountains of choice, serving up traditional turkey with all the trimmings, rounding it off with pumpkin pie and lashings of cream.

AUSTRALIA DAY
AUSTRALIA

 nationwide holiday in the grand land of Oz, Australia Day is a public holiday for the entire country. On January 26 each year, all Australians take a day to consider just what it is that makes their country special to them. It wasn't always like this as for many years, different parts of the country celebrated at different times.

Australia Day marks the anniversary in 1788 of the arrival of the First Fleet of 11 convict ships from Britain. As they arrived, Captain Arthur Philip raised the Union Jack at Sydney Cove. Although modern day Australians mark the past, today's celebrations are more about contemporary Oz, its achievements and future opportunities.

Some sections of the community, particularly the indigenous people, have objected to the celebrations and have to tried to rename it Invasion Day, with little support. It's a day for families, for community fun and partying. Don't forget that late January is high summer down under, so many celebrate outdoors with barbecues and picnics and fabulous fireworks displays.

Wherever you happen to be in Australia - from Perth to Sydney, Brisbane to Melbourne, there will be celebrations you can join in with. Many music festivals are planned for the day. Often there are special one-off sports games and bars and restaurants festoon themselves with the Australia flag, offering a great range of national dishes all washed down with some of that famous amber nectar!

fun

PARTYING

Places to See before you die...

MONUMENTS

ST BASIL'S CATHEDRAL
MOSCOW, RUSSIA

Its massive collection of onion-shaped globes soaring into the Russian sky makes St Basil's Cathedral one of the most appealing monuments in the country.

This tremendous architectural feat will literally take your breath away, and that's even before you have set foot inside. The huge cathedral was built by Ivan the Terrible. He wanted it to commemorate the capture of the Tartar stronghold of Kazan in 1552.

The cathedral has nine different chapels, each with its own different sized dome. Each chapel is said to mark a victorious assault on the city of Kazan. It is named after the 'holy fool' Basil the Blessed, who was very popular with Moscow folk and even with Ivan the Terrible himself.

If you're on a tour of Moscow, St Basil's is easy to find. You can see it from miles around and it sits in Red Square, close to the Kremlin. Step inside to marvel at the fantastic collection of historical artefacts from St Basil's time.

The place is home to a museum and you can also get an idea of how the clerics would have lived back then, in tiny cells with low roofs and narrow corridors.

Once outside, you must have your picture taken against the backdrop, it is one of the most popular and iconic shots for any tourist visiting Russia, so go with the flow and smile!

GOLDEN GATE BRIDGE
SAN FRANCISCO, USA

The Golden Gate Bridge is one of the most recognisable bridges in the world. It spans the Golden Gate Strait, a 3 mile (4.8 km) long mass of water that connects the grand Pacific Ocean to San Francisco Bay.

It took over four years to build, but San Franciscans had been dreaming of having a bridge for over 100 years before construction started. Hundreds of men were involved in the project which started in 1933 and finally opened to vehicles in 1937.

The bridge is gorgeous to look at. Despite its name it is actually painted in orange vermilion with a suspension span of 4,200 feet. On its opening day, the San Francisco Chronicle described it as a '35 million dollar steel harp!'

The bridge provides a vital link between Highway 101 and Marlin County, thousands of cars and other vehicles use it every day. Even with six lanes of traffic, it gets very congested. You can travel across the bridge in a vehicle for a small toll fee. Pedestrians can cross it free of charge, which is a great way to savor the views across the Bay area.

No matter what time of year you travel, you should be able to cross the Golden Gate without problem. The bridge has only been closed three times in its lifetime, all down to perilously high winds.

savor the wicked VIEWS

with

sculpture with WOW FACTOR

MOUNT RUSHMORE
SOUTH DAKOTA, USA

These massive sculptures hewn into the rock at Mount Rushmore are testimony to the dedication of an army of craftsman. It has become a shrine for the people of the USA, a memorial and monument to the country's growth and ideals.

You'll have seen pictures of it dozens of times before, but nothing replaces the sense of awe you'll feel when you come face to face with the four 60-foot busts of some of the greatest American Presidents. This is a sculpture with wow-factor! As well as marvelling at the granite faces, there is also a museum and Avenue of Flags where every single one of the US states is represented.

The presidents carved in stone are George Washington, Thomas Jefferson, Theodore Roosevelt and Abraham Lincoln. Together they represent the first 150 years of American history. This quartet of leaders is credited with putting in the groundwork required to make the US the leading world power that it is today.

You'd think this was the work of a younger man but sculptor Gutzon Borglum was 60 when he started drilling into the side of the mountain in 1927. At the time it was known as the Shrine of Democracy and took 14 years to build.

Each of the four presidents' heads is as tall as a six-storey building, their noses are 6 m (20 ft) long and each eye spans 3.3 m (11 ft). Mount Rushmore Memorial is situated in the heart of Black Hills and as well as the museum, there is a Presidential Trail so you can get the best views of the great men.

STATUE OF LIBERTY
NEW YORK, USA

Better than a bunch of flowers or a box of chocolates! The French gave the Statue of Liberty to the Americans in 1886 as a thank you present for the friendship established between the two nations during the American Revolution. Nowadays, the Statue of Liberty is seen as a symbol for a bigger message: of friendship, freedom and democracy for the American people.

It was actually a joint project, the Americans were responsible for the plinth and the French designed the statue to go on top. Sculptor Frederic Auguste Bartholdi came up with the huge copper structure and completed it in time to commemorate the 100th anniversary of the American Declaration of Independence. It is said that the face of the statue was modelled on his mother Charlotte.

A trip to New York must include a visit to Liberty. You need to take a ferry to get to the island and numbers are carefully controlled. Most people just visit the plinth and surrounding grounds. You can actually take the steep climb inside Liberty upto her Crown, but these get booked up months in advance. It's not for the faint-hearted either, if you hate small spaces and heights then it's best to admire it from the outside.

The trek to the crown involves climbing 154 steps. While you're there, check out the American Wall of Honor which features over 700,000 names of dozens of nationalities, including people forced to migrate from slavery and the very earliest settlers.

spreading

THE

NEWS to

NEW

YORKERS

EMPIRE STATE BUILDING

NEW YORK, USA

Soaring high into the New York skyline, this Manhattan skyscraper is the most recognisable building in the Big Apple. It teeters a staggering 443 m (1,454 ft) into the air and attracts thousands of visitors every year.

If you can handle heights, then go for the tour that takes you to the observatory on the 86th floor. If you're even more daring, you can soar to the 102nd floor for a true bird's eye view of the city.

Few people have the stamina to make the 1,860 steps to the 102nd floor and opt for the lifts. When you bear in mind its colossal size, it's astonishing to think that the Empire State Building took just over a year to build.

It's set on the site of the old Waldorf-Astoria Hotel and was officially opened by President Herbert Hoover on May 1, 1931. With the tragic demise of the Twin Towers, it remains the tallest building in the Big Apple.

The building is illuminated for high days and holidays and in the days before mass communication, was used as a way of spreading news to New Yorkers. The first light to shine on top of the building was to show that Franklin D Roosevelt had been elected as President in 1932.

The Empire State Building has featured in many motion pictures throughout history, including King Kong, An Affair to Remember and Sleepless in Seattle.

NOTRE DAME CATHEDRAL
PARIS, FRANCE

 soaring testimony to the art of gothic architecture, Notre Dame Cathedral dominates the skyline of France's capital city, nestling on its own Île de la Cité, in the River Seine.

The cathedral, whose name means Our Lady of Paris, is the most visited tourist destination in France, with over 13 million visitors each year. The current building stands on the site of an earlier religious church.

When it was deemed to be the parish church of the Kings of Europe, Bishop Maurice Sulley decided that a grand new construction was required and so the Notre Dame was born.

As you wander through the wondrous building, you will spot many styles which prove that several different architects have worked on the place over the years.

During the French Revolution, many treasures were plundered and the cathedral was used as a warehouse to store food. The Virgin Mary was taken down and replaced by Lady Liberty on the altars.

It's free to enter the cathedral but there is a small charge if you want to visit the Tower or Treasury. It's one of those places that you can research avidly or just let yourself wander the aisles and marvel at the craftsmanship and history within.

dominates the SKYLINE

GUARANTEED

 MaGNifiCENt

view

EIFFEL TOWER
PARIS, FRANCE

By rights, the Eiffel Tower shouldn't still be standing. This delicate-looking fretwork tower was only intended to be around for 20 years but was saved by scientific experiments and the fact that it came in very handy as radio transmission and telecommunication innovations grew.

The tower bears the name of its creator, Gustave Eiffel, who was commissioned to create a masterpiece for the 1889 Exposition Universelle, to celebrate 100 years since the French Revolution.

It may look flimsy from afar, but the Eiffel Tower is extremely solid and well worth the effort it takes to climb. There are stairs for the hardy and lifts for the lazy! The tower has several stopping places on the way to the top and wherever you rest you are guaranteed a magnificent view of the whole of Paris and beyond, on a clear day.

If you want to delve deeper in to its history, you can take a guided tour that includes the original engine rooms still powering the lifts today. And if you get peckish, there's even a restaurant on the first floor where you can dine with breathtaking views of the city from your table.

At night, the tower is illuminated and brightens up the Paris skyline for all to see. Every evening, for five minutes in every hour, it sparkles with lights, giving off a bewitching golden glow.

The eye-catching design has spawned plenty of mimics over the years. The best-known and oldest impersonator is Blackpool Tower, built in 1894. You will also find replicas in Las Vegas, Paris, Tennessee and Paris, Texas! There are even two Eiffel Tower copies in China and another in Tokyo, Japan.

ST. PETER'S BASILICA
ROME, ITALY

This stunning structure is considered one of the holiest sites in the history of the Christian church. It stands on the site where Peter, the apostle considered to be the first Pope, was crucified and buried. His tomb lies under the main altar and the Basilica is the final resting place of many other popes.

Don't let anyone tell you it's a cathedral, it's not! In Rome, that honour goes to the Basilica of St. John Lateran. St. Peter's was founded by Constantine in 324 AD but was rebuilt in Renaissance times with the expertise of such masters as Bramante, Michelangelo and Bernini.

St. Peter's stands on St. Peter's Square, the beautiful piazza with its two sparkling fountains and central obelisk. If you think churches are dusty and dull, then think again! St. Peter's will simply blow you away! Once you step inside, you'll be astonished by the incredible craftsmanship within.

St. Peter's has the largest dome in the world and the longest nave. Even if you are not religious, you'll be mesmerised by the atmosphere and air of spirituality that exudes throughout the place.

There are plenty of guided tours you can take around St. Peter's, but many who have visited before say that one of the best things to do is to find a quiet place to contemplate the beauty and spirituality of this great building.

LOPSIDED

VIEW

OF THE

CITY

LEANING TOWER OF PISA

PISA, ITALY

It looks like it should have toppled over into a heap years ago, yet the Leaning Tower of Pisa still stands and is one of Italy's most recognisable landmarks. When you get there, you'll probably find yourself leaning over too, in an attempt to work out just why the structure manages to stay roughly upright!

No-one knows what made engineer Bonanno Pisano carry on with the construction when things looked pretty wobbly, but he did, and over 800 years since building started, it still stands.

The leaning tower was a particular embarrassment for the people of Pisa. At the time, the city was seen as a centre of military might and artistic excellence, so the building really wrecked their street credit.

Pisano designed the 56 m (186 ft) tower and started building it on a foundation of soft sand, rubble and clay. You don't have to be a civil engineer to guess that something a little more solid would have been preferable.

As the building grew, it settled unevenly, but work carried on. To make up for it, builders began to make each new tier a little higher on the short side, but this just made the tower sink more.

Adding a bunch of bells in the tower made it sink even lower and by the late 1990s, the tower was leaning a even more at 5.2 m (17 ft) to the south. You can see this feat of engineering for yourself and for a small fee you can climb to the top for a lopsided view of the city.

TAJ MAHAL
AGRA, INDIA

Shah Jahan must surely qualify as one of the most romantic men on the planet. After the love of his life, wife Mumtaz Mahal died, he dedicated the rest of his life to overseeing the building of this magnificent palace in her memory.

Effectively, the Taj Mahal in all its glory is a memorial to the dead. It's a real love story and anyone who stands in front of the fantastic building can't fail to be moved by its size and splendour. It is now designated as one of the Seven Wonders of the World.

It all began back in 1607, when Prince Khurrum fell in love with a beautiful girl and they became engaged. Five years on, they married and had lots of children. Prince Khurrum went on to become Emperor Shah Jahan and his wife was known as Mumtaz Mahal.

Things went desperately wrong when she died giving birth to their 14th child. Devastated Shah decided that the Taj Mahal would be built in her memory and once completed it became one of the most breathtaking places on earth.

This amazing building, fashioned entirely out of white marble, is also decorated with a host of precious and semi-precious stones. Over a thousand elephants and 22,000 workers were involved in building the Taj Mahal, which took 20 years to complete.

A real LOVE story

of

EDINBURGH CASTLE
EDINBURGH, UK

This massive fortress sits in a commanding position on top of a huge volcanic rock overlooking Scotland's capital city. The site is steeped in centuries of myths and legends. It is even supposed to have its own ghost in the form of a lone piper who is said to mournfully trail round rooms and passageways.

Records show that people have inhabited the site for hundreds of years, but for Edinburgh, the Middle Ages were its heyday. The city grew up around the castle, with the oldest houses closest to the imposing stronghold, leading down the High Street to the Royal Palace of Holyrood House. This stretch is known as The Royal Mile, in honour of the many trips Royals would make between the two locations.

Make sure you're at the castle around lunchtime for the One O'Clock Gun. It's a tradition from the days when it was used as a time signal for ships in the Firth of Forth and the port of Leith. The Gun was first fired in 1861 and has been fired six days a week at 1pm ever since, except during the two World Wars.

Inside it's a real treat for the eyes. The most popular exhibits are The Honours of Scotland (the crown jewels). The crown, sceptre and sword of state are housed in the Crown Room, which was built specially for them way back in 1617 when King James VI returned to the country to celebrate his Golden Jubilee.

Treat Edinburgh Castle as the focal point of your stay in this wonderful city. The place is home to a vast array of marvellous architecture and if you're there during August, head to the grounds in front of the Castle for the Edinburgh Military Tattoo, a colourful display of British and ceremony at its best.

PRAGUE CASTLE
PRAGUE, CZECH REPUBLIC

ou're guaranteed to be astonished by the beauty of the Czech Republic's top tourist attraction. This amazing collection of buildings is the biggest castle complex in Europe and was home to the Czech monarchy through the ages. It is more than a castle though, it's a massive complex comprising three courtyards and many other buildings including the towering St. Vitus' Cathedral, several palaces, towers and even a monastery.

If you're on a tight budget and just want to soak up the atmosphere, you can wander round the courtyards free of charge. However, to get a real feel for the way people lived, buy a ticket and take a tour. Once inside, you will sense history all around you.

There have been many changes to the buildings over the years and the complex is testimony to the ever-changing fashions in architecture and decor. Back in the 9th century a castle was erected on the site to be replaced by a Romanesque palace 300 years later. Gothic styles became popular during the 14th century and yet more changes were made after a fire in the 1500s.

As you wander round, you get a clear view of the different eras. Nowadays, there is no royal family in the Czech Republic and the castle is the seat of the President instead. Every hour during the day, the changing of the guard takes place, but make sure you get there for 12 noon when there is a fanfare too!

sense

of HISTORY

all AROUND

JOURNEY

TO the

top

GATEWAY ARCH
ST. LOUIS, MISSOURI, USA

This vision in steel is the USA's tallest monument. At 192 m (630 ft) high, it's one of those things you just can't stop staring at. But looking at it from ground level is just half the experience.

The Gateway Arch was created over 40 years ago by Eero Saarinen and was commissioned to commemorate Thomas Jefferson and the city of St. Louis' role in the way the western side of the USA developed. It is filled with lots of attractions, including the breathtaking Journey to the Top, movies and plenty of opportunities to shop.

If you're really daring, you can take the Journey to the Top in an enclosed tram. The trip takes four minutes but the memories of the sights you'll see will last a lifetime! While you're there you can watch two movies, chronicling the story behind the creation of the Arch.

While you're in St. Louis, take a look at the Museum of Western Expansion which tells the story of native Americans as well as the pioneers who set out to tame the old West.

If you have seen the movie Percy Jackson and the Lightning Thief, the Gateway Arch will be instantly recognisable. In the film, Percy is attacked by Chimera at the very top of the Arch and forced to jump out of a window into the water below.

Rest assured, that was all fiction and safety precautions are very thorough and robust!

BASILICA CISTERN
ISTANBUL, TURKEY

We know what you're thinking: how on earth can a system that supplies water be on your list of things to see before you die? However, this isn't just any old rusty tank, this is one of the most gorgeous hidden treasures in the whole of Istanbul.

The Basilica Cistern, also known as the Sunken Palace or Yerebatan Sarayi, is a fascinating example of ingenuity from hundreds of years ago. When you get down there you'll be astonished by the workmanship, especially when you consider it was built in 532 AD!

The Basilica Cistern is massive, over 135 m (453 ft) long and has a staggering 336 marble columns, some of which are decorated with the upside-down head of Medusa. No one is quite sure why she is the wrong way up!

It is named after the huge square it was built underneath and legend has it that over 7,000 slaves were used to help construction. If you're a fan of James Bond movies, the Basilica Cistern will look familiar as it was used in the 1963 film From Russia with Love.

Don't worry, you don't have to get wet to look around. Though it has the capacity to store 100,000 tons of water it is quite shallow these days. Plus, walkways have been installed so that you can travel through the Cistern without even a splash.

gorgeous

hidden

TREASURES

PETRONAS TOWERS
KUALA LUMPUR, MALAYSIA

At 452 m (1,482 ft), these twin towers are some of the highest in the world, connected by a high bridge. You can take a trip up the towers in the lift, but once you're up high you have only a few minutes to snap your pictures before you have to head back down.

The towers are named after Petronas, short for Petroliam Nasional, Malaysia's national petroleum corporation. Tower One is fully occupied by their offices, with Tower Two let out to other companies.

Together the Towers weigh the equivalent of 60 grown male elephants. They stretch into the sky for 88 storeys and 765 steps of stairs. Fortunately, to save people's legs, each tower has 10 escalators and 29 large lifts.

With the tragic demise of New York's Twin Towers, they are the now the tallest twin skyscrapers in the world. In keeping with Malaysia's mainly Muslim tradition, the outside of the buildings feature motifs that are found in historical culture.

The towers are joined by a sky bridge on the 41st and 42nd floors. If you want some really amazing views, you can access the sky bridge but it is a big attraction in Malaysia and only 1,000 people a day are allowed to cross it. You can also travel as far as the 86th floor.

It's reassuring to know that the sky bridge has also been designed as a safety device, so if one tower needs to evacuate, people can cross to the other side. The Towers featured in the 1999 film Entrapment, which starred Sean Connery and Catherine Zeta Jones.

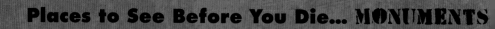

SYDNEY OPERA HOUSE
SYDNEY, AUSTRALIA

One of the most recognisable buildings in the entire world! It pays homage to Australia as a seafaring country with the roofs of the Opera House depicting a ship in full sail. This landmark building has the amazing triple accolade of being a State, National and World Heritage landmark.

Back in the 1950s the government of New South Wales launched a competition for someone to design an opera house. Danish architect Jorn Utzon came up with such a fantastic design that no one was sure if his dreams could become reality. It was a stressy time and eventually work started, with the building being finished by others in 1973. Queen Elizabeth II performed the official opening in that year and it has become a symbol to everything new and innovative that Australia stands for.

But don't just look at it, beautiful though it is. Get inside! The Sydney Opera House hosts more than just operatic events and while you're there, book yourself tickets whatever is on at the time. There are many performing spaces, from an opera theatre, drama theatre, studio, playhouse and several other areas. So much goes on, every year there are around 1,700 performances enjoyed by 1,250,000 visitors.

You can take a number of tours, from an engrossing tour with a plot to rival an opera, to the fascinating backstage tour showing you all the nuts and bolts needed to put on a show that audiences remember forever!

a SHIP IN fUll SAIL

TICKING

BIG BEN
LONDON, UK

Big Ben is one of the most recognisable monuments in the UK and a timeless feature of the big New Year's Eve countdown. The huge clock tower is part of the Houses of Parliament, and even though we all call it Big Ben, this is actually the name of the massive bell inside the tower.

The colossal clock is quite breathtaking at any time of day, but particularly awesome at night when all four faces are lit up. When parliament is in session, an additional light is shown above the clock face to show that MPs are sitting.

Big Ben's timekeeping is regulated by a stack of coins which are placed on the huge pendulum and it has hardly ever stopped working. Even after a bomb decimated the chamber of the House of Commons during the Second World War, the clock kept on ticking.

Though it looks like a real piece of very old history, Big Ben isn't quite as old as you might think. The original Palace of Westminster was destroyed in a fire back in 1834. When time came to rebuild, the new seat of parliament was redesigned to include a tower and a clock. Big Ben struck for the first time in 1859.

Though you can take a tour of the Houses of Parliament, the clock tower, which houses the massive bell called Big Ben, isn't open to the public. However, if you live in the UK, you can write to your MP at the House of Commons and ask them to arrange a visit, but make sure you plan your trip well ahead.

Places to See before you die...

CULTURE

LOUVRE MUSEUM
PARIS, FRANCE

More than just the home of the Mona Lisa, this massive museum houses treasures from all over the world. The Louvre used to be a royal palace but has been a museum since the end of the 18th century. It is situated right in the heart of Paris, in a gorgeous setting surrounded by formal gardens known as the Tuilieries.

King Francis I started the collections as a private exhibition for the personal pleasure of the royal family. He bought the Mona Lisa and the collection grew steadily. It was first opened to the public in 1793 during the French Revolution.

The newest addition to the buildings of the Louvre is the Louvre Pyramid, constructed entirely of glass which acts as a dramatic entrance to the museum.

So what else is there to see inside? Join the queues to see the enigmatic smile of Leonardo da Vinci's Mona Lisa. She only became truly famous when the picture was stolen from the museum in 1911 and it was another two years before she showed up again. The theft cost the museum's director his job.

There is also the famous sculpture of Venus de Milo and the Dying Slave by Michelangelo. Plenty of exhibits are on show year round and the museum also holds many temporary events.

treasures

from all over the WORLD

STRATFORD-UPON-AVON
WARWICKSHIRE, UK

The home of William Shakespeare, the most famous playwright in the world, this beautiful riverside town of Stratford on Avon has something to offer everyone. Nestling in rolling countryside in the heart of England, Stratford oozes the Bard from every pore.

There are numerous opportunities to immerse yourself in all things Shakespearean. The Royal Shakespeare Company is based right in the centre and puts on many of William Shakespeare's plays every year.

There are five houses in and around Stratford connected with Shakespeare and his family and they are all well worth a visit. All the houses date from the 16th century and are crammed with artefacts from that time. Shakespeare's Birthplace, a wonderful half-timbered house, is the most visited.

Take yourself away from the bustle of the shops and bars of the town centre to visit Holy Trinity Church where both William Shakespeare and his wife are buried. The church itself is a fab example of intricate architecture and its courtyard and cemetery exude beauty and peace.

There is more to Stratford-Upon-Avon than Shakespeare though! The river is home to an enormous colony of swans and you can take a river trip to view the town from the water. Because the town is so well preserved, a wander round the streets is a must.

Among the places worth visiting, there is a shop called the Trading Post, which used to be a gaol with a cage for prisoners, and the White Swan Hotel which was a public house back in Shakespeare's time.

FLORENCE CITY TOUR
FLORENCE, ITALY

The gorgeous city of Florence, or Firenze in Italian, is credited with being the place where the Renaissance began. And it is truly gorgeous, crammed with historical places, paintings and sculptures. In fact it is so hard to decide what to see that UNESCO has made its entire centre a World Heritage Site.

You could stay a month and still not see everything the city has to offer! However, even if you are just there for a couple of days, it's easy to cram in some of the most desirable sites. Florence is the capital city of Tuscany and has been a key location for centuries.

One of the best places to start your tour is at the cathedral, the Duomo or Santa Maria del Fiore, to give it its proper name. This is an awe-inspiring Gothic structure with a massive dome, the largest of its kind when it was built. You can climb to the top of the dome by trekking up 463 steps and once there take in a breathtaking view of the historic city.

No trip to the city is complete without a visit to Ponte Vecchio, the stunning covered bridge that crosses the River Arno. A short walk away, you'll find the stunning Uffizi Gallery, which is crammed with Renaissance masterpieces including Botticelli's the Birth of Venus.

Finally, if you run out of time, just take a seat at a café table and look around you, after all, Florence isn't known as an open air museum for nothing!

PLENTY
OF
interaction

HEINEKEN & RIJKSMUSEUM

AMSTERDAM, HOLLAND

The first part of this trip is definitely for the grown-ups! This tour involves beer so you have to be over 18 to enter as the entrance price includes two drinks. A great way to learn more about brewing, this Amsterdam attraction is more than a museum as it offers plenty of interaction as you go round.

Set in Heineken's old brewery, it's a fun way to learn more about beer-making and sample a sip or two at the same time! For years the brewery, a landmark building in Holland's industrial heritage, produced millions of litres of beer until it moved to a new site. Among the attractions are a mini-brewery and a tasting bar. You can also take the Stable Walk to visit the company's magnificent shire horses that still deliver beer around the city.

If you're in Amsterdam for a couple of days, make time for the Rijksmuseum. It has been in existence for over 200 years and was established by the King of the Netherlands, Louis Bonaparte (Napoleon's brother). The building itself will take your breath away and houses some of the finest paintings and artworks by many of the Dutch masters.

These include Rembrandt's Night Watch along with several paintings by Van Dyck, Vermeer and Jan Steen. But the collections aren't just Dutch, there is a vast array of Asian art, an enormous collection of prints and classic photography.

Allow yourself plenty of time to get round the Rijksmuseum. It's a place where you are allowed to linger for as long as you like. And you'll probably find yourself spending money in the museum's three shops, buying postcards of some of the classic paintings you've just seen!

WEST END SHOWS
LONDON, UK

ondon's West End is home to some of the most spectacular shows on the planet. At any one time there can be as many as 200 different shows to choose from, including performances to make you laugh, cry or scared witless.

Whether you want an over-the-top musical or an intimate play in a Victorian theatre, prepare to be spellbound! There are theatres dotted all over the West End, from the imposing Apollo, to the stunning London Palladium, to the historic theatres that line the streets of Drury Lane and Shaftesbury Avenue.

The West End is a great place to see your favorite performers up close and personal. Many TV stars sign up for a stretch on the boards to hone up their dramatic skills and re-connect with the intimate world of live performance.

If you want to sign up for a spot of history, take yourself to see The Mousetrap, Agatha Christie's murder mystery play. When it opened in 1952 it starred Richard Attenborough and it has been running continuously ever since. Though the West End is revered for its musical prowess, don't neglect straight stage plays. Many top Hollywood stars have taken part in limited runs of classic plays, including Kevin Spacey, Vanessa Redgrave and Jeff Goldblum.

prepare

to be

SPELLBOUND

HOLLYWOOD WALK OF FAME
LOS ANGELES, USA

Take a stroll down Hollywood Boulevard to do your own star-spotting, literally. Forget holding your head up high when you stride out, for this one you need to keep your head down at pavement level! It's a tribute to over 2400 stars who have made Hollywood the greatest movie-making place in the world, from actors and actresses to fictional characters, directors and musicians.

Wherever you start on Hollywood Boulevard, you'll spot a star. They are either made from brass or from terrazzo in a gorgeous candy floss shade of pink. There are stars all along the pavements on both sides of the street for 15 blocks of the Boulevard and several blocks of Vine Street.

If you're lucky you might even get to see a new star being laid in a formal induction ceremony! The Walk can get incredibly crowded, after all it attracts a staggering 10 million visitors a year, all searching for the star belonging to their favorite performer. Immerse yourself in the atmosphere, you'll be surprised at just how much fun it is!

The first star was placed in February 1960 for the actress Joanne Woodward. Though it doesn't really matter where you start your walk, most people recommend the Four Ladies Gazebo at La Brea.

The list of stars is endless but includes masses of big names from over 100 years of showmanship including Houdini, W.C. Fields, the Lone Range, Bette Midler, Elton John, Greta Garbo, Steve McQueen and Burt Reynolds.

You can also spot the handprints of Hollywood stars outside Grauman's Chinese Theatre forecourt.

GUINNESS STOREHOUSE
DUBLIN, IRELAND

Ireland's top visitor attraction pays homage to the dark velvety drink that is synonymous with the country. Even if you've never tried a glass of Guinness, you'll find the storehouse a fascinating experience. The Storehouse takes visitors through the origins of the brand at the historic building in St. James' Gate all the way to the present day with the famous Guinness harp logo easily identified across the world.

It's an ingenious attraction and begins at the Storehouse Atrium, which is the shape of a giant Guinness glass stretching up through the centre of the seven-storey building. You get to learn about the brewing process and how four simple ingredients, water, hops, yeast and barley are transformed into the alcoholic drink.

But it's more than a mere brewery tour. You also get to learn about the art of the cooper, the men who made the barrels to transport the black drink across the world. Today Guinness is shipped to over 150 countries and over the years every kind of transport imaginable has been used, from horses, to barges, trains, planes and ships.

So many people have Irish heritage that it's worth checking out the genealogy section. The Storehouse keeps as many records as possible of people who worked at the Brewery from 1759 to the present day and before you go, you can fill in a form that could help trace their working details. When you've completed the great tour, what better way to round off your trip than with drinking a glass of it at the Gravity Bar, which offers fantastic views over Dublin.

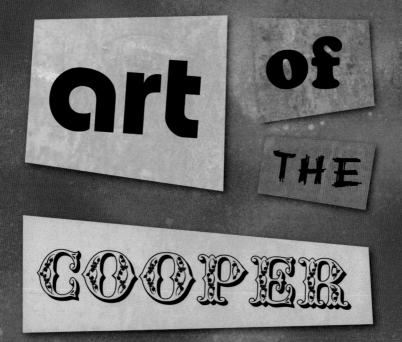

FROM

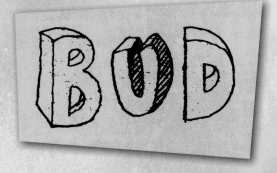

BUD

TO

bloom

NAPA VALLEY WINE TOUR

CALIFORNIA, USA

The heart of California's winemaking industry, Napa Valley is home to dozens of vineyards of all sizes. From massive operations covering swathes of the gorgeous countryside to small, single grape wineries, there is something for every wine lover and many ways to see the world of winemaking at work.

Napa Valley is a stunning area of California and depending on the time of year you go, the landscape will offer something different. The place is awash with mustard in late winter and vines at different stages the rest of the year, from bud to bloom.

The main wine-making towns include Castiloga, St Helena, Napa, Yountville, Oakville and Rutherford. There is a tour to suit every budget, from cycling to stretch limousine! You can even take the Napa wine train to see the sights.

Most wineries offer tours and wine tastings. You can opt to make your own way there or join an organised tour which will take you to a range of wineries that produce red, white, rosé and even sparkling wines.

You don't have to be a wine connoisseur to enjoy the experience. The Napa Valley is renowned for its friendly people and the whole area is geared up to making your stay a memorable one, whatever your budget.

The warm climate of the area also makes Napa a popular destination for people who just want to chill. There are plenty of spa experiences around so if you just want to relax after all that wine tasting, you'll have no problem at all!

ABORIGINAL TOUR
AUSTRALIA

If you're Down Under, leave the city behind for a while to investigate the cultural heritage of the country's original inhabitants – the Aborigines. There are plenty of organised tours available to take you beyond the stereotypical views of the Aborigines as colourful dancers and cave artists.

Depending on where you are based in Australia, you can take anything from a one-day tour to a longer trek with overnight stops Among the choices are a one-day trip from Cooktown, Queensland, led by a Nugal-warra Elder which takes in several rock art sites including the Great Emu Cave. Steep yourself in the history of Aboriginal art and learn more about their survival techniques.

For a longer tour you can take the Ten Canoes trip which offers a real glimpse into the lives of the indigenous people of the Northern territory. You will meet up with Aboriginal guides who offer you the chance to hike, fish and hunt, collecting native foods, which you then cook and eat.

If you haven't got the time to take a specific tour, then head for the country's museums. Sydney, in particular has a wealth of Aboriginal artefacts in many of its galleries, particularly The Australian Museum and the Yirbana Gallery of New South Wales, home to one of the largest collections of indigenous art and sculpture.

leave

the city

BEHIND

VATICAN MUSEUMS
ROME, ITALY

These museums, inside the Vatican City, are some of the finest in the world, attracting over four million visitors every year. Established by Pope Julius II in the early 1500s, they contain thousands of pieces chronicling the history of the Roman Catholic Church and many Renaissance pieces and renowned masterpieces.

It's safe to say that you simply won't have time to see everything here, mainly because there is so much to see. With every step, you will spot something else worth looking at! The area includes the breathtaking Sistine Chapel with its stunning ceiling painted by Michelangelo and Raphael's Stanza Della Segnatura.

Must-sees include the Chapel of Beato Angelico, the Raphael rooms and the Borgia Apartment. Among the areas particularly worth looking at is the Gallery of the Candlebra, crammed with impressive Roman sculptures. Absolutely mesmerising is the Gallery of Maps which features 40 topographical maps of Italy.

You're guaranteed to get neck ache while going round the museums as almost every ceiling is painted with dazzling frescoes depicting Biblical scenes. Though much of the stuff on show is hundreds of years old, there are plenty of more modern pieces to see.

Take a look inside the Borgia Apartment. This was a private wing built for Alexander VI at the end of the 15th century. The rooms there are now used to house the collection of Modern Religious Art – a fabulous mix of paintings and sculptures by artists including Gaugin, Chagall, Klee and Kandinski.

MONTMARTRE
PARIS, FRANCE

ne of the most colourful areas of Paris, Montmartre was originally a village for artisans situated close to the city. Today it is home to many street artists and creative types and has a buzzing atmosphere and thriving artistic community. Montmartre is situated on a hill. Its name means mountain of the martyr in honour of Saint Denis, who was decapitated on top of the hill back in the year 250 AD.

The area became known as a free and easy place to be after Emperor Napoleon III drove out some of Paris' original inhabitants, forcing them to find a new home in Montmartre. They quickly established their own 'town,' which flourished without rules and regulations. Bars and nightspots sprang up, the most famous of which is the Moulin Rouge, which attracted many customers with its saucy can can dancers.

By the mid 1800s, artists began to treat the place as home. Pissarro was one of the first to settle there, followed by stars like Edgar Degas, Henri Matisse and Pablo Picasso. Today, Montmartre is a designated historic area and retains much of its historic charm. The best way to explore is on foot. Or, you can hop on the funicular railway that takes you up the hill to the world famous church of Sacré Coeur. Here you can sit on the many steps and take in what must be one of the best views of Paris.

When you're tired of sightseeing, settle down in one of the many little pavement cafes and do what the French do best, watch the world go by with a cup of coffee or glass of wine!

without

RULES

and

REGULATIONS

NEW YORK ART

NEW YORK, USA

A trio of museums, the Guggenheim, MOMA and Met, are all situated in the heart of New York City and are all worth a look for different reasons. Whether you are there for a couple of days or a longer stretch, make sure you take time out to visit some of New York's finest art displays.

The Guggenheim is an architectural work of art in itself. The building was designed by Frank Lloyd Wright and is dedicated to displaying the best of 20th century art and beyond. It has numerous collections including notable works from such masters as Picasso and Chagall.

MOMA (the Museum of Modern Art) is also in Manhattan. The idea for such a place came from Abby Rockefeller and her friends Lillie Bliss and Mary Quinn, back in 1928. They rented a small space and opened their museum in 1929. The place grew into the success it is today. Among the works on show are Andy Warhol's iconic Campbell's Soup Cans, The Dance by Matisse, Number 31, 1950 by Jackson Pollock and Rousseau's The Dream.

The Met (Metropolitan Museum of Art) was founded in 1870 and is now one of the world's largest art galleries. It's a wondrous cornucopia of stuff, and includes a fantastic collection of musical instruments, costumes and wondrous accessories.

Here you can admire paintings, dream of being able to dress in some of the divine creations and get a real taste for treasures from all over the world. One of the most popular exhibits is the Arms and Armour gallery, featuring a parade of army figures on horseback.

CHAMPAGNE TOUR
CHAMPAGNE, FRANCE

It's the fizz of celebration, a delicate bubbly drink that many other countries have tried to imitate but failed to improve on. The Champagne region in France offers a huge variety of tours. You can opt to visit the well-known Champagne houses such as Epernay or Veuve Clicquot or choose to take a tour of the smaller ones.

To be called Champagne, this sparkling wine must be produced from grapes grown in the Champagne region. The main grapes used are Pinot Meunier, Pinot Noir and Chardonnay. Champagne is synonymous with luxury, its association with celebrations and all things grand dates back to the anointment of French kings.

In France it was known as the 'devil's wine' after bottles exploded, forcing the cork out! For years it was made using a basic method and it wasn't until the 19th century that the official 'methode champenoise' became commonplace.

You'll find out even more on a Champagne tour and may even find your luggage considerably heavier with bottles on your way home. You can take a day or a week but a two-day trip to Reims or Epernay can fill you with plenty of fizz knowledge, its history, harvest and production.

The top places to start is Reims, home to many houses including the much revered Taittinger. Cheers!

of

celebration

THE KING OF ROCK 'n' ROLL

GRACELAND
MEMPHIS, TENNESSEE, USA

The home of The King of rock 'n' roll, Elvis Presley, Graceland is a mega-tribute to the man credited with making pop music what it is today. It's a fascinating trip, one you should make time for, even if you're not a fan. A tour through this massive southern mansion will take you from Elvis Aaron Presley's humble beginnings through to his rise to super stardom until his untimely death at the tragically early age of 42, in 1977.

As well as a homage to the man himself, Graceland takes you through the history of modern America and that makes it all the more fascinating. It covers the country's big, brash heyday of the 1950s and 1960s and shows just what the world's biggest superstar did with all the money he earned.

Among the exhibits on show are a 1958 Convair jet, named Lisa Marie after his daughter. Take a look inside at the true celebrity interior complete with a toilet suite flecked in 24 carat gold! Elvis adored cars and 33 of them are on show including his famous Pink Cadillac, a 1975 Ferrari and even a John Deere tractor that he used on his ranch.

Aside from all the glitz and glamor, you get a real insight into the man and his family life. Elvis lived here with his wife Priscilla and daughter and you can imagine him doing everyday things, from eating breakfast in the kitchen to relaxing on the sofa watching TV.

Graceland is also home to an amazing collection of trophies and discs which serve as proof, if any were needed, of Elvis' huge success. There is also a dazzling collection of his stage outfits! The final stop on your tour will be the Meditation Garden where Elvis and members of his family are buried.

WONDERS

GRAND CANYON
ARIZONA, USA

One of the most recognisable natural wonders in the world, this amazing canyon was carved by the passage of the Colorado River. The Grand Canyon is 277 miles (445 km) long,. Most of it is in the Grand Canyon National Park and around five million people a year make the trek to visit this amazing spectacle.

You can go for the day or stay for a while, the canyon is home to many official camping grounds. Most people choose to see the Grand Canyon from the South Rim. This is the most accessible part of the park and is open all year round. You can also check it out from the North Rim, but this is harder to get to and is often closed from October to May due to snowfalls.

If you're fit and hardy you can explore the Inner Canyon. To do this you need to hike, hire a mule or take a river trek, all of which take longer than a day. If you have time on your hands and have worked out at the gym, this offers one of the most mind-blowing experiences around. From the Inner Canyon, you get to experience the place close up, a memory to cherish forever.

Alternatively, you can take a bus or hire a car to take the Desert View Drive, a stunning trip which follows the South Rim and has plenty of stop-off viewpoints along the way. Inevitably, for a site so memorable, the Grand Canyon has appeared in many films, most notably the finale of Thelma and Louise starring Geena Davis and Susan Sarandon.

memory

to CHERISH

forever

NIAGARA FALLS

NEW YORK, USA & TORONTO, CANADA

These amazing Falls are the most powerful in North America. They form the international border between Canada and the US state of New York. The Falls are actually two major sections separated by Goat Island, the Horseshoe Falls on the Canadian side and the American Falls on the US side.

They would have formed when glaciers receded during the last ice age and the Great Lakes carved a path through on their way to the sea. The Falls were already a popular spot for US and Canadian honeymooners and the number of tourists increased massively after Niagara, a 1953 film starring Marilyn Monroe hit the cinemas.

The Falls can be viewed from both sides, but the Canadian side is most popular, attracting around 25 millions visitors a year. Although many visitors view the Falls from high up, one of the most popular attractions is the Maid of the Mist boat tour, which takes visitors close up to the Falls on the water.

The Falls have become a holiday destination in themselves, no longer just a quick day trip. Go on the Journey Behind the Falls, which takes you 150 feet down a lift to a bedrock behind the falls, which allows you to experience the feeling of being behind such a powerful force of water.

As you might imagine from such a phenomenal natural attraction, there are plenty of places to stay, along with restaurants, even casinos and a giant Ferris Wheel so you can admire the view from the air.

AMAZON RAINFOREST

SOUTH AMERICA

If you've always wanted to visit the Rainforests of the Amazon basin, then think about doing it sooner rather than later before the ecosystems of the area disappear in a wave of development. This really is one of those areas where it's worth taking a guided trip led by people who have in depth local knowledge of the area.

One of the best ways to see all the best of the Amazon is by water. You can choose to raft, kayak or take a dugout canoe. The Amazon really is a once in a lifetime trip, a mesmerising mix of ecosystems and hidden cultures. These days you can really get close to Amazon life, choosing to trek with experienced guides, including shaman who can guide you through the fascinating mix of flora and fauna that abound at every turn.

Most reputable tour companies ensure you get a range of accommodation, from very basic tents to eco-friendly cabins. Many offer plenty of expertise on plant and animal life in the Amazon, and some even introduce a cultural exchange between tourists and the indigenous tribes for whom the Amazon is home.

There is often the wondrous opportunity to also explore Amazon cloud forests. These tours are frequently guided by expert naturalists who can talk you through the habitat featuring hanging ferns, rare orchids and a colourful array of bird life.

UNDERWATER

BOX OF treasures

GREAT BARRIER REEF

AUSTRALIA

One of the Seven Wonders of the World, this amazing reef off the coast of Australia is home to the world's largest coral reef. Thousands of species of marine life thrive here and the area encompasses over 3,000 smaller reefs, coral cays and tropical islands. The Great Barrier Reef is absolutely colossal. To give you an idea, it is longer than the Great Wall of China and the only living thing on earth that is visible from space.

There are masses of ways to experience the reef, you can see it from the air on specially arranged flights, take a boat or if you are a qualified diver or into snorkelling, you really can get up close and personal by going deep under the ocean's surface.

Head to Queensland and treat one of the seaside cities as a base. Cairns is one of the best centres to explore the Reef from but there also smaller towns such as Townsville, Rockhampton and Mackay which offer plenty of accommodation to return to after sampling delights of this underwater box of treasures.

If you have money to burn there are several island retreats including Heron Island, deemed to be fantastic for scuba diving and snorkelling and a great place to go turtle and whale watching. At low tide you can also take reef walks where you can see some coral formations first hand.

The reef is home to many rare species, including the endangered Dugong (Sea Cow) and the Green Sea Turtle. It's a truly fabulous place to visit, even if you're not a diver. After a busy day exploring, local restaurants specialise in seafood and local delicacies as you watch the sun go down.

VICTORIA FALLS
ZAMBIA & ZIMBABWE

The world's largest curtain of water, known as the 'smoke that thunders' sits on the Zambezi river, bordering the countries of Zambia and Zimbabwe. Officially they are in no man's land. The Falls are over 100 m (328 ft) high and 1.25 miles (2 km) wide and the noise of the water cascading down can be heard from afar.

Scottish missionary David Livingstone is thought to have been one of the first non-Africans to see the Falls in the 1860s and he named them in honour of Queen Victoria who was on the throne at the time. They attract thousands of visitors each year, many from the local area. Unlike many natural attractions, the Falls are easy to get to by public transport!

There are two islands close on the crest of the Falls and they are large enough to divide the massive curtain of water, even at full flood. One of these is called Livingstone Island and is the place where Livingstone had his first sight of the wondrous waterfall. Not surprisingly, the area is home to plenty of watersports and adventure activities. You can even do a bungee jump there!

Don't expect the place to be full of restaurants and flash hotels, the Victoria Falls have escaped much of the commercialism that has grown up round other amazing world heritage sites. Either side of the Falls are national parks to preserve the area. Further upstream there are tranquil lagoons inhabited by hippos and crocodiles. Combine a trip to the Falls with a safari to really make this an unforgettable experience.

smoke

THAT

THUNDERS

extraordinary

NATURAL

phenomenon

GIANT'S CAUSEWAY

COUNTY ANTRIM, UK

An extraordinary natural phenomenon, it's no wonder people believed that a giant really could have walked along this amazing causeway. It features 40,000 polygonal basalt columns, some as high as 12 m (40ft). Experts believe it's the result of a series of volcanic eruptions 60 million years ago but local legend is much more fun, with tales of battling giants deemed to be the root cause.

The Giant's Causeway is near the town of Bushmills, famous for its Irish whiskey, and is both a UNESCO World Heritage Site and a National Nature Reserve. It's Northern Ireland's most popular tourist attraction. It is possible to walk on the site with the tops of the columns acting as stepping stones.

When you get there, have a bit of fun and see if you can identify different shapes within the Causeway itself. Years of weathering mean that you can pick out things that resemble objects, including the Giant's Boot, the Camel's Hump, the Chimney Stacks and the Giant's Harp.

The Causeway is now owned by the National Trust. It is open year round and there are plenty of gorgeous walks along the coastal path that borders the stones. If you're feeling energetic, there is plenty of information locally on longer walks in the area.

While you're admiring the views, keep a look out for an amazing array of sea birds, including petrels, cormorants, guillemots and razorbills. Down by the shoreline you might spot rock pipits and eider duck have been known to frequent the sheltered water where the Causeway sinks into the sea.

128

AYERS ROCK
NORTHERN TERRITORY, AUSTRALIA

This massive red sandstone monolith erupting from the ground is steeped in magic and mystery and will leave you with lasting memories of its beauty and simplicity. Ayers Rock or Urulu, is situated in the heart of what has become known as Australia's Red Centre. To the indigenous people, it is the country's spiritual heart and has great meaning to the lives of Aborigines.

Plan to spend more than a day in the area, because, in addition to Ayers Rock there is its sister rock Kata Tjuta nearby with the stunning King's Canyon close to Alice Springs.

Ayers Rock rises 348 m (1,141 ft) from the desert. A vision of different shades of red, it matches the light and the weather with such amazing colours that locals say it can upstage the sunset.

There are plenty of tours in the area, and if you want to know more about its spiritual significance, join a group led by one of the Anangu, the local indigenous people who are happy to share details about the flora and fauna of the area, as well as tell traditional stories.

It is possible to climb Ayers Rock but you need to be pretty fit to attempt it as the going is steep and can be windy. If climbing is not your game, there are plenty of other activities for you to take part in the area from riding a camel to hiring a Harley, Easy Rider style!

STEEPED

in

MAGIC

and

mystery

a thing of HEAVENLY beaUty

ANGEL FALLS
VENEZUELA, SOUTH AMERICA

The world's highest falls are hidden away in the highlands of Guayana in Venezuela. They are 15 times higher than the Niagara Falls with a cascade of 979 m (3,211 ft). The Falls are caused by water from the River Churum tipping over the edge of Auyantepuy Mountain.

You'd be forgiven for thinking the name comes from the fact that they are a thing of heavenly beauty. In fact, they are named after an adventurous American pilot. Jimmy Angel spotted the waterfall for the first time in 1933 while searching for something completely different, the McCracken River of Gold.

He came back four years later but had engine troubles and was forced to make an emergency landing high up on Auyantepuy. He and three companions had to abandon their plane, walking back to civilisation on an 11-day trek through the jungle. His plane stayed stuck at the top for 33 years and is now on show at the Aviation Museum in Maracay. A replica sits at the top of the mountain as a memento.

The falls are in the heart of the Canaima National Park and are one of the country's top tourist attractions. You have to be pretty determined to see them though. The most popular way to see them is by river trip and tourists usually need to fly in to reach Canaima camp, the starting point for most trips.

Guides are experienced and very knowledgeable about not just the falls, but also the flora and fauna of the area. Seeing the falls in person is a wondrous experience. Even though the falls are the highest in the world, the water flow can seem quite limited, especially as much of the water disperses as mist on the journey to the river below!

NORWEGIAN FJORDS
NORWAY

These visually stunning creations were formed in successive ice ages when the glaciers retreated and the water flooded U-shaped valleys. Norway has the largest concentration of fjords in the world, with the highest number of them in western Norway.

You'd be forgiven for thinking that the climate in the area would be chilly to say the least. But because of the Gulf Stream, the fjords actually have a mild climate and hardly ever get iced over. If you're lucky you will see seals basking in the area, and a wealth of amazing bird life, including the majestic eagle.

The best way to experience these fjords is by boat and the villages of Gudvangen and Geiranger are the most popular cruise ship ports in Scandanavia. If you're worried that too much tourism will spoil the experience, then think again. The Norwegians have gone to great lengths to ensure that the fjords remain as unspoilt as possible.

If there was a year-round place to go, then this is it. Most people visit the fjords in the summer months when daylight lasts for hours. But locals recommend autumn as one of the best times to visit, when the changing colours of falling leaves are reflected on the glass-like surfaces of the fjords. Spring is also a riot of colour with flowering trees in full bloom. Even in winter, you'll find it quite mild, though you will definitely need waterproofs and an umbrella!

VISUALLY

STUNNING

creations

broken

into three

parts

SPLIT MOUNTAIN

GAETA, ITALY

In itself, Gaeta is a wonderful old seaside town, the perfect place to relax and just enjoy the scenery. But thanks to myths, legend or reality, it is more than that. Gaeta is home to Split Mountain (Montagna Spaccata), a rock promontory that is said to have broken in to three parts at the death of Christ.

To get to the mountain, you have to go through the Sanctuary of the Holy Trinity, a monastery complex. There is a charge to get through but it is worth it. It's a lengthy walk, full of steps that take you between two of the splits down close to the sea.

Take it steady and you will come up to the tiny chapel of S. S. Crucifix. Among the things to look out for is a large hand print in the rock. According to local legend, a Turk didn't believe the story of the mountain splitting and said that if it were true the rock would liquefy, leaving his handmark!

Follow the signs for the Grotta del Turco (the Turk's Grotto). The cliffs overlooking the sea are split in half, all the way from top to bottom. You can take the path down to the grotto, it's a tricky walk, especially in the wet, but well worth it. The grotto itself is a natural wonder, carved out of the mountain by the erosion of the sea.

As well as the Split Mountain, Gaeta has seven gorgeous beaches, the most popular of which is Sant'Agnostino, known for its rich sunsets. Local churches are also seeped in significance, most notably the Golden Chapel in the Annunziata church which was made famous by Pope Pius IX when he officially announced the dogma of the Immaculate Conception here in 1854.

HA LONG BAY

QUANG NINH PROVINCE, VIETNAM

A fantastic spot with so many beautiful natural wonders colliding in one space. It's renowned for its water, caves and grottoes and the weather also gives rise to some enthralling cloud formations to finish off the scene.

The limestone creations are all shapes and sizes and along with the bay itself they form what is now a UNESCO World Heritage site. There are hundreds of tiny limestone islands and towers in the bay. Some of them are hollow and feature caves.

As the weather in Ha Long is tropical monsoon-style, the best time to visit is during the summer months when most activities are available and rich blue skies form a clear backdrop to the bay.

One of the best ways to experience the beauty of the area is by water and many boats offer tours. Some include the opportunity to visit off-the-beaten track lagoons using easy-to-navigate kayaks for part of the journey.

You'll be fascinated by the colourful floating fishing villages that exist all the way round the bay. Ha Long Bay itself is home to plenty of hotels and places to eat. Not surprisingly, local fish dishes top the menus. Also worth a look is Ha Long market, worth a trip for the hustle and bustle of locals busy at work!

enthralling CLOUD formations

WONDERFUL

NATURAL

CREATIONS

REDWOOD TREES

CALIFORNIA, USA

If you thought California was all about Hollywood and beaches for the rich and beautiful, then think again! Tucked away in the north of the county are some of the most wonderful natural creations around: the Giant Redwood Trees.

The county is home to many of the surviving redwoods in the world and they flourish here in a protected environment of three state parks, along with the Redwood National Park. Together, the parks form a World Heritage Site and an International Biosphere Reserve.

The National Park is home to the world's tallest tree Hyperion, at over 115 m (379 ft). Redwoods can live for 2000 years and grow on average to about 109 m (360 ft). Because of their height, numerous other species grow beneath them and these parks have plenty of variety of other trees and shrubs including spruce, hemlock and the feathery sword ferns.

Exactly how you choose to experience the Giant Redwoods is up to you and there are lots of ways to do so! Prairie Creek Redwoods State Park offers perhaps the widest choice. You can take a scenic drive through the park or opt for going on foot. There are 75 miles (120 km) of treks for all levels of ability. You can always choose to go on two wheels as there are plenty of biking options. You can even hire a horse and trek through the parks, taking a tasty picnic with you!

The parks aren't just about the trees and plants. There are stacks of opportunities to spot wildlife, including elks and spotted owls. The area is home to over 250 different species of animals!

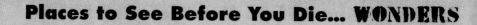
MATTERHORN
SWITZERLAND

This enormous mountain is a real symbol of Switzerland and believed to be one of the most photographed mountains in the world. Its name means meadow peak, thanks to the fantastic flourishing of spring flowers that form a carpet across it in the spring. It rises to 4,478 m (14,692 ft) and is famous not for its height but for the fact that its four faces point in the exact cardinal directions of north, south, east and west. The first ascent was in 1865. A team led by Brit Edward Whymper managed the ascent but three of them were killed on the way down.

Unless you're an experienced climber, used to trekking up bare rock and using crampons, then it's probably best to admire the Matterhorn from afar. The mountain has claimed the lives of 500 climbers, and even today around 12 people every year are killed trying to complete the feat.

Zermatt is a car-free village at the base of the Matterhorn, which during ski season is one of the places to be seen. It's also worth taking a look at the Klein-Matterhorn (the Little Matterhorn), situated next to its big brother. You can board an aerial cable car in Zermatt that takes you up the smaller mountain to the highest station in the Alps.

The Matterhorn also lends its name to the Matterhorn Gotthard Bahn, an Alpine railway which offers some of the best travelling views in the world. The line starts in Zermatt and takes you through the Alps, passing through 33 tunnels and over 100 bridges and viaducts on the way, the trains being immaculate and always running on time!

FANTASTIC

flourishing

of SPRING

flowers

RICH IN legend

BLUE GROTTO

CAPRI, ITALY

Steeped in history, this is one of the highlights of any trip to Europe. The Blue Grotto (La Grotta Azzurra), takes some determination to visit and is not for the claustrophobic. Entrance is only by boat and you have to lie down in order to squeeze through the narrow arch that takes you inside.

Once inside the grotto, there is plenty of room to sit up and admire the way the light plays through the water to create the intense blue. The place is rich in legend. In Roman times, Emperor Tiberius was said to have used the place as a marine chill-out zone and there are still Roman statues inside.

The blue colour comes from the way that sunlight passes through the seawater and shines through an underwater cavity. The place was revealed to the world in 1826 by German writer August Kopisch and over the years it has become the symbol of the tiny island of Capri. Not surprisingly, the Grotto is out of bounds during rough weather as the entrance to the cave is less than a metre high.

If you decide against going by boat, it is possible to swim into the grotto if you leave it until the end of the day when the boats have gone. Always check weather and tide times before taking this option.

Aside from the Grotto, Capri is a fabulous place to spend a few days. It has long been a centre for artists and creative types. Gracie Fields, who had a hit with the 1934 song The Isle of Capri, had a villa on the island and singer Mariah Carey also has a home there.

AURORA BOREALIS
VARIOUS LOCATIONS

Seeing this amazing natural light show is a jaw-dropping experience that will live with you forever. Also known as the Northern Lights, the Aurora Borealis are best spotted in the late autumn/winter and early spring, high up in the northern hemisphere. One of the best places to see them is said to be above the Arctic Circle in northern Norway, Iceland, parts of Sweden and in the north west territories of Canada.

It is never possible to predict a sighting, but the longer you stay in the area, the better chance you have of seeing this fantastic sky show. The best advice is to avoid full moons, which make the display paler. Lights can appear any time after dark between 6pm and 1am from the autumn to spring equinoxes (September 21st to March 21st).

These flickering bands of ever changing iridescent green lights, sometimes tinged pink and purple, can appear several times in one night or stay away for days. Patience is paramount and it is likely to be pretty cold, so wrap up warm! In Greek mythology, Aurora is the goddess of the dawn and the lights were seen as her way of renewing her energies before the morning's work.

Not surprisingly, the lights have been the source of many superstitions. Hundreds of years ago, when they could be seen from as far south as France and Italy, people believed they were omens signifying death.

fantastic

SKY

Show

SALTIEST sea

IN THE

world

THE DEAD SEA
ISRAEL

This amazing natural wonder is the lowest and saltiest sea in the world! It is known as the Dead Sea because its high salt content means that no life forms can exist there. Though it is known as a sea, it should really be called a lake. It is bizarre that a place where no life can survive has a reputation for providing many health properties to the people who visit.

The composition of salts and minerals in the water are renowned as having positive health benefits. The seabed is also coated in thick black mud, which people believe is good for the body. Check out any picture of the Dead Sea and it's likely to feature someone coated in the black stuff! Jump into the waters and enjoy the amazing floating sensation, thanks to the high salt content, you can loll around floating for as long as you like!

There is more to the area than the waters though. All around the lake there are tourist beaches and some specially designated for therapeutic purposes. There are also some amazing monasteries in the area, dating back from the fourth century when early Christians wanted to live as Jesus had. The Judean desert became a popular destination for Christian monks, who built fascinating monasteries in the area, many of which you can look round.

The Dead Sea is an area with accommodation to suit all budgets, from the most luxurious hotels to hostel accommodation. As it is close to the desert, it is a great base to learn more about the indigenous Bedouin tribes who still live in the region. The more daring of you can take jeep or camel tours, but for those who like their trips more refined, the Dead Sea is also a great spot for museums and art galleries.

Places to See before you die...

ADVENTURE

GREAT WALL OF CHINA
CHINA

The only man-made structure visible from space took over 2000 years to build. Like a dragon with a long swishing tail, it winds its way across all manner of terrain, from deserts to mountains and grasslands for a massive distance of around 5,500 miles (8,851 km). Some parts of the wall have disintegrated or are in the process of being restored but it is possible to walk long parts of it, starting from a number of locations.

It was constructed by several different Chinese emperors, starting in 475 BC. The aim of the wall was to keep out their enemies, particularly the Huns. When members of the Ming Dynasty got involved between 1368 and 1644 AD the wall started to get much more elaborate. They added all sorts of fancy pieces including watchtowers, bridges, battlements and cannons.

The width of the wall varies between 4.5-9 m (15-30 ft) wide, certainly wide enough for two cars to drive on side by side. Many parts of the wall are accessible to visitors and providing you're reasonably fit, you can trek. If you're just trying to incorporate a Wall visit with a trip to Beijing, it is possible to take day trips to key areas of the site.

The most visited part of the Great Wall is in Badaling. It was the first part of the Wall to be opened to visitors in 1957 and it made a spectacular finishing point for a cycling course at the 2008 Olympics.

VISIBLE

from

SPACE

AMAZING

INSTINCTIVE

journey

WILDLIFE MIGRATION
KENYA & TANZANIA

The massive annual migration of millions of wildebeest, zebra and other antelope in East Africa has to be seen to be believed. Every single year around 1.5 million and 300,00 zebra, along with a host of other antelope, make the long journey from the plains of Serengeti in Tanzania to the Masai Mara National Reserve in Kenya.

This amazing instinctive journey is around 1,800 miles (2,896 km) long and fraught with danger. Their aim is new pastures for food and water. Every year around a 250,000 animals die on the way.

Among the most fascinating sights is when the animals form a massive moving line to cross the Grumeti River in Tanzania and the Mara River in Kenya. This usually happens any time between July and September and claims the most victims of the trip.

As the thousands of animals trek across the plains, they attract all kinds of hungry beasts, including crocodiles, lions, leopards and hyenas, who follow the migration and pick off any animal that gets separated or can't keep up with the crowd.

Because migration is a natural event, you can't predict exactly when the animals will start their trek. Whether you choose to watch the migration from Kenya or Tanzania, you need the expertise of tour operators in the area to make sure you can do so safely.

INCA TRAIL
PERU

Take an Inca trail through Peru to the Lost City of the Incas and let the memories of this hidden world will live with you forever. Machu Picchu lies high in the Peruvian Andes and is the highlight of any Inca trek. Known as the Lost City, it remained undiscovered, hidden for centuries until the American archaeologist Hiram Bingham revealed his find to the world in 1911.

Taking an Inca trail calls for an early start, steep climbs and rocky descents in the high altitudes of South America, so you'll need plenty of grit and determination. Tours are run by guides with masses of experience, about both the terrain and the potential problems of trekking at high altitude.

En-route to your final destination you will get to experience the vibrant life of Peruvian towns and villages. With any luck you will be able to watch the sun rise against mountain backdrops and perhaps get the chance to relax aching limbs in one of the area's many thermal springs.

This trip calls for plenty of pre-planning, the most important thing of all is to make sure you are fit for the challenge. Only 500 people a day are allowed through the trail that leads to Machu Picchu and permits are arranged through tour operators. As it's one of the most popular treks in the world, plan at least three months ahead.

CENTURIES

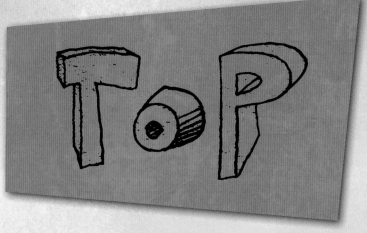

MOUNT KILIMANJARO
TANZANIA

You need stamina, fitness and sheer push to climb what is known as the 'Roof of Africa', a trek to the top of Mount Kilimanjaro. Kili, as it's known is said to be one of the world's most beautiful mountains. It's best to make sure you are physically fit before you book.

The mountain, which is the highest in Africa, has three volcanic cones: Kibo, Mawenz and Shira. It towers in at 5,895 m (19,340 km). For years, it has beckoned adventurous types into its midst. Many years ago only mountaineers attempted the climb, but now it has become accessible to anyone with the determination to keep going.

The first European to conquer Mount Kilimanjaro was a German professor called Hans Meyer. He completed his climb in 1889 accompanied by Austrian Ludwig Purtscheller and a Marangu Army Scout Kinyal Lauwo. Since then hundreds of others have achieved their dream.

A trek up Mount Kilimajaro can take you through all four seasons of the year in as many days, from lush spring plants through to the snow and ice as you near the summit. Depending on which trip you choose to take, there are six routes up the mountain.

The best way to enjoy the climb is to listen to the advice of the experts you go with. Since 1991, all trekkers are only allowed to make the climb if they book with a licensed agency. Ask anyone who's got to the top though and they'll tell you the sense of achievement is immense. Never mind being on the roof of Africa, they feel like they are on the top of the world!

KENYA SAFARI

KENYA

One of the top things on people's lists of things to do is a safari to Kenya, which evokes thoughts of great excitement. Unlike the safaris of yesteryear which consisted of one man driving a dusty old bus, the safaris of today can be as luxurious and detailed as you like.

Nowadays there are many operators in the business offering tailor-made safaris, from luxury lodges or base camps with all modern conveniences. There are still more rough and ready alternatives available, though. It's up to you!

On safari, most people want to see the 'big five', but these days there is much dispute over which five should be included! Many years ago it was the lion, leopard, black rhino, elephant and cape buffalo.

However, the 'big five' can be anything you want it to be. Everyone has their own must-see animals. Most people like to get a glimpse of giraffes on their safari, and hippopotamuses come top of many people's lists. You may end up seeing lots of things you never expected to as you travel through the game reserves.

Kenya is a huge country and the choice of safaris is immense. One of the best ways to experience the sight of wildlife is to go for a trip that offers a mixture of accommodation, from tented camps to safari lodges.

thoughts

of **great**

EXCITEMENT

ROAD TO SANTIAGO

SPAIN

This major pilgrimage route was one of the most important during medieval times. It is also known as the Way of St. James. According to legend, St James' remains were carried by boat from Jerusalem to northern Spain, where he was buried in what is now the cathedral of Santiago del Compostela in Galicia.

Traditionally the route began from the pilgrims' home all the way to Santiago and in the Middle Ages it was a hugely popular trip for Christians. Over the past few years, there has been a massive resurgence in pilgrims making the trek along what has been recognised as a European Culture Route and also a UNESCO World Heritage Site. Around 25,000 completed the route in 2010, deemed a holy year as St James' Day fell on a Sunday.

There are several routes to Santiago and they can all be adapted to suit the amount of time you have to spare. These include two French Routes that begin in the Pyrenees and either take you to Roncesvalles through Navarre or Somport through Aragon. Both routes converge in Puente la Reina and continue towards Santiago.

You need to have a reasonable level of fitness to make the trip, but there are plenty of organised tours that allow comfortable stop-offs en-route. Some will even transport your bags for you. You don't have to be particularly religious to take this journey and no matter what your reasons, you will find it a richly rewarding experience and undoubtedly meet many other pilgrims on the way.

SKIING DELUXE
CHAMONIX, FRANCE

This gorgeous French location was the site of the first Winter Olympics in 1924 and has long been one of the most popular skiing destinations in the world. Chamonix is situated close to the peaks of the Aiguilles Rouges and shares the summit of Mont Blanc with the Italian village of Courmayeur just over the border.

If you have a head for heights then you will love it! Chamonix is famous for its cable car, which whizzes passengers up the Aiguille du Midi and is the highest cable car journey in the world. In the summer, when the snow is mostly melted, the place is a mecca for mountaineers and also mountain bikers, who have a wonderful maze of tracks to test their nerve.

The Chamonix Valley is home to five ski resorts and collectively they have the reputation of being up there as offering some of the best skiing around. There are runs for all levels of ability, from beginners, to experienced skiers and those who want real thrills by skiing off piste.

When you need a break from skiing there are lots of ways to enjoy the stunning scenery and clear mountain air. One way to get close to the massive peaks is to board the Montenvers train, a funicular railway that climbs from the valley floor to the impressive Mer de Glace glacier. There is plenty for wildlife lovers too, from marmots to mountain hares and if you're very lucky, you may spot the very private and rare lynx!

mecca

for

MOUNTAINEERS

CAPE HORN
HORNOS ISLAND, CHILE

The bane of many a sailor's life, Cape Horn, located at the southern-most tip of the American continent, used to be seen as a challenge to the many seamen who had to confront it. When the Panama Canal was built, it saved many from the undoubted risks of traversing this headland.

For hundreds of years, Cape Horn has been known as the sea of fear and for many years it became the norm to plunder ship-wrecked boats in the area, rather than offer any assistance. Cape Horn rises as a huge black rock and the waters around it are home to thousands of shipwrecks and countless victims.

Among seafaring folk, it is said to have the worst weather on the planet, yet people still crave the experience for themselves. The waters around the Horn and the archipelago of islands just to the north, can be home to several different types of weather in the space of a day, from rain and winds, to sun, snow and even ice.

The most famous ghost ship said to haunt the area was captained by a man who became known as the Flying Dutchman, due to his erratic behaviour. Trying to round the Cape in appalling weather, he refused to take advice from his men and went below to drink and smoke. When a mutiny broke out he shot the ringleader and threw him overboard. The ship was never officially seen again.

After all that, one of the best ways to see the Cape is still by boat. Not surprisingly, many of the trips that take you round the Horn start from Chile or Argentina. They are well planned, but be prepared for seriously unpredictable weather!

BASE CAMP
NEPAL

Follow in the footsteps of the great climbing parties who were drawn to tackle Mount Everest, at 8,848 m (29,028 km), the world's highest mountain. The magnificent mountain exerts a pull over adventurers like no other place, but to actually trek to the summit requires years of preparation and a high degree of risk.

The mountain scenery as you trek through the hilly terrain of Nepal is absolutely spectacular. Experienced Sherpas, who know the region inside out, will be with you all the way and you get to learn a lot about their culture in the process. The trek to Base Camp is challenging because of the high altitudes you'll be walking through. And days are long but the rewards are immense.

The best place to start is the vibrant city of Kathmandhu, you'll then travel to one of several starting points for the trek. There are plenty of trips out there to suit your budget but you need to allow yourself a good few days to acclimatise and complete the trek. As you might imagine, you won't be staying in luxurious accommodation, but what you miss out in terms of comfort you'll make up for in the memories you're left with and the friendships you make.

Mount Everest Base Camp isn't something you can zip up and down in a few hours. There are acclimatisation stops on the way to ensure you're body is handling the physical demands of the trek. Before you go, make sure you can handle a seven hour walk without any problems, and you'll be in a strong position to make the most of the real experience.

rewards

are 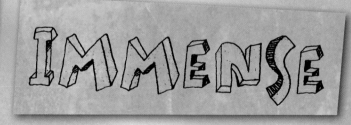 IMMENSE

VAST

EXPANSE

 OF natural

COUNTRYSIDE

YELLOWSTONE
NATIONAL PARK
WYOMING, USA

The world's first national park, Yellowstone National Park is a vast expanse of natural countryside spanning a huge area of Wyoming and edging slightly into Idaho and Montana. It is home to all kinds of wildlife.

The wildlife is high on most visitors' lists with elks, bison and two types of bear making their homes here, though the bears are in fact shy creatures and stay well away. There are also moose and several packs of wolves, which have gone on to breed successfully after being reintroduced to the park a few years ago.

The park also has the largest active geyser field in the world, Old Faithful. This was discovered back in 1870, by members of the Washburn Expedition who stumbled on it as it erupted. Today, this giant geyser erupts every 90 minutes or so, shooting warm water into the air. It is worth spending half a day in the geyser field to be in with the chance of seeing an eruption or two!

There is also the breathtaking Grand Canyon of Yellowstone and plenty of chances to take part in adventure sports, from white water rafting to horse trekking through the wonderful scenery. There are 1,300 miles(2,092 km) of trails for you to take on foot, offering treks that take a mere hour, to lengthier journeys that require a whole day.

If you're not feeling energetic, rest assured there is a road network that passes through the Park so you can still see an awful lot even if you've forgotten your walking boots!

GLACIER TREKKING
SWITZERLAND

This sounds like a seriously scary activity, but you'll be surprised to know that it's something many people can tackle, provided they are reasonably fit and steady on their feet. You can take day trips but the Swiss experts recommend that you try a two-day hike to really make the most of your beautiful surroundings

One of the most popular hikes is down the Aletschgletscher, Europe's largest glacier at around 14 miles (22 km). It's situated in an area that is one of UNESCO's Greatest Wonders of the World. You hop on a train from Grindelwald or Lauterbrunnen. It's a superbly scenic ride that takes you to Jungfraujoch, the highest railway station in Europe.

Glacier trekking is a great addition for the adventurous. If you're on a standard skiing trip and fancy something a little different then it's worth a try. If it conjures up ideas of slithering on sheet ice, then think again! Glaciers have varying types of terrain, your guide will make sure you are prepared before you start.

When you come down to earth, make sure you dig into some yummy, traditional Swiss delicacies: a taste bud-tingling cheese fondue or raclette, which is Swiss cheese drizzled over potatoes. Tuck in with abandon, you'll have earned it! If you fancy something sweet, then it would be wrong not to sample some of the chocolates that have made Switzerland famous, while resting those aching limbs in the comfort of pristine, Swiss accommodation.

superbly scenic RIDE

luxury

travel of

YESTERYEAR

ORIENT EXPRESS
ASIA & EUROPE

Immortalised by Agatha Christie in her famous mystery novel: Murder on the Orient Express, this train journey sums up luxury travel of yesteryear. Originally a long distance passenger railway, the Orient Express served the great cities of Paris to Istanbul. Today, the new Venice-Simplon Orient Express continues to run this journey of a lifetime, using carefully restored carriages from the 1920s.

Nowadays, there is a choice of locations. You can still travel to Paris and Istanbul, but the service has opened up, as the name suggests, to include Venice and other European cities. Sit back and revel in the romance of a golden age. You'll travel in style with Lalique glass panels, wood burning stoves and intricate art deco relief.

You can rest in vintage cabins, dine on superb cuisine or simply sit back and take in the scenery as the train rushes on its elegant journey across Europe. You'll be seeped in history just sitting on the train. Each carriage has been lovingly restored and has its own story to tell. One carriage was stuck in a snowdrift for 10 days in 1934, another was shot at during the Second World War and a third was used to transport European royalty!

Treat the journey as a holiday in itself or combine it with a stay in any number of cities, from Venice, to Paris, Budapest and Bucharest. Whatever you do, you'll be in good company! The train features in several books and films: in 'Bram Stoker's Dracula', the group sworn to destroy him take the Orient Express. James Bond has a fight with a rival on the train in 'From Russia With Love'. Rest assured, your journey will be a little less dramatic!

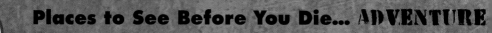

ANGKOR WAT
SIEM REAP, CAMBODIA

This absolutely stunning temple was built in the 12th century for King Suryavarman II as his state temple. It is one of the largest Khmer monuments and features on the national flag of Cambodia. From Angkor the Khmer kings ruled over an enormous area that stretched from Vietnam to China to the Bay of Bengal.

The temple is unusual in that it faces west, whereas most other temples in the city of Angkor face east. Over the years, the temple has changed its devotions. Originally it was dedicated to the Hindu god Lord Vishnu but by the 15th century it was converted to a Theravada Buddhist temple.

The place is steeped in mysticism. Angkor Wat symbolises Mount Meru, a mythical mountain and it has five walls and moats that represent mountainous chains and the oceans of the cosmos. The name Angkor Wat literally means City Walls.

Astonishingly, when you consider how long ago it was built, the complex's dimensions are aligned precisely along a north-south axis. The world's largest religious building is an area of such staggering beauty that you can't fail to be impressed.

Step inside and admire the beautiful illustrations depicting scenes from Indian literature, including dragons, griffins and warriors. This awe-aspiring building is sure to take your breath away, inside and out!

STEEPED

IN

mysticism

TEA & HORSE TRAIL
CHINA

The Silk Road linking the cultures of the East and West is one of the most significant routes in all of history. Less well known, but just as important is the Tea & Horse Trail that spans over 1,429 miles (2,300 km) across China and into Sichuan, Tibet as far as India and Nepal.

As far back as the 10th century, this vibrant trade route linked China, India and Burma. Traders stopped at outposts on the route to exchange not only commercial goods but traditions as well. In the Yunnan part of China they transported blocks of tea to trade for horses that had been bred in Tibet. Even today the area is a rich mix of cultures and traditions.

The Tea & Horse Trail consisted of two main routes, each coming from major points of tea production, in Yunnan and Sichuan, before converging and continuing into the arid landscapes of Tibetan plateau. Isolated tribes relied on the route to exchange goods and referred to it as the Eternal Road.

Unless you have weeks at your disposal it would be impossible to undertake the whole journey but it is now possible to take a guided trip to the Yunnan province to retrace part of the journey. Depending on who you choose to go with, you can hike through portions of the road or let buses take the strain. It's a wonderful opportunity to sample the local traditions of the area and get the opportunity to sample some of China's delicate teas.

China is gradually opening up as a tourist destination to visitors from the west and this is a trek that promises to give you a glimpse of China and its trading routes that few others will have seen!

BLUE LAGOON
ICELAND

 eed a spot of pampering? Need a lot of pampering? Either way, you've come to the right place at the Blue Lagoon, one of the most visited attractions in Iceland. Even if it's cold outside, the geothermal waters of the Blue Lagoon are warm and inviting, thanks to the effects of lava formation.

Its warm waters are rich in minerals like silica and sulphur. The lagoon, which is surrounded by Blue Flag beaches, is wonderfully relaxing. You can soak up the warmth of the water while breathing in the fresh, clean air from the Icelandic hills.

As well as being plain lovely, the waters are reputed to be helpful for people with certain skin conditions and there is a research centre on site to help find treatments. However, be warned as Iceland is strict on hygiene and insists that everyone showers without clothing in a communal area before using the lagoon.

Free silica mud is provided for all guests and you can rent essentials like towels, swim wear and bath robes. You can opt to enjoy the waters or really indulge by booking any of the usual range of spa treatments.

It's easy to find and just 40 minutes or so from Reykjavik, Iceland's capital. Regular buses make the journey there and there is also a hotel and restaurants so that you can extend your stay to enjoy the therapeutic benefits of the Blue Lagoon for a little longer.

RICH IN minerals

 living

FILM

THROUGH THE ROCKIES
TORONTO, CANADA

A real epic journey across Canada and what better way to enjoy it than to let the train take the strain while you sit back and admire the wonderful views. Linking the lovely cities of Toronto to the sea port of Vancouver, this is one of the world's most popular long-haul train journeys. It really is a trip on a grand scale.

It takes four days to travel between Canada's largest city and Vancouver on the Pacific coast and the views are constantly changing, like a living film reel. You will cross an immense boreal forest, pass the lakes of northern Ontario then head through the western Prairies onward through the great mountain range of the Rockies. Along the way, you will pass through some of the country's major cities including Jasper, Edmonton, Saskatoon and Winnipeg.

To reflect the length of time passengers spend on board, the carriages have undergone a massive refit to make sure travelling is truly comfortable and there are plenty of choices to suit all budgets. Travelling by train is a cool way to relax. The stresses and strains of getting somewhere evaporate the minute you find your seat. All there is left to do is relax and enjoy your surroundings!

It's also a good idea to give yourself time to explore the cities at each end. Toronto is home to the massive Eaton Centre with over 250 shops, the 553 m (1,815 ft) CN Tower and plenty of museums and galleries. Vancouver has been voted one of the best cities in the world to live in. It includes a terrific range of shops and restaurants and is home to many landmarks including the peaceful Stanley Park and cruise ship port Canada Place.

ROUTE 66

USA

Immortalised in the song of the same name, now it's time to follow in singer Bobby Troup's footsteps and take this modern day pilgrimage across the USA from east to west. Yes folks, it's time to get your kicks on Route 66! A popular jaunt for people from all over the world, Route 66 is said to sum up everything about the country, from freedom, to expansion in to the West, to the loneliness of America's heartland.

People who have done the trip before recommend you give yourself plenty of time, at least nine or ten days to be able to make the most of the scenery and stop at places on the way. Though you will pass through plenty of built up areas, some parts are still quite remote, with petrol stations as much as 100 miles (160 km) apart, so make sure you're well stocked with fuel, food and water.

The old Route 66 is not on modern maps but there are plenty of companies out there who produce the old-style maps to ensure that you can stick to the proper trip. Most people take what is also known as the Mother Road from east to west, but feel free to be contrary and do it back to front, ending up in Chicago.

You can choose to book up motels and hotels in advance or just go for it, it's normally quite easy to find a satisfactory bed for the night after a good meal in a local diner. You can vary your route slightly but whichever way you go you will be putting in over 2,000 miles (3,218 km) from start to finish.

HISTORIC

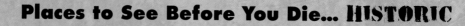

IMPRESSIVE

EVEN

IN

ruins

THE COLOSSEUM

ROME, ITALY

This is probably the most recognisable building left standing from the days of ancient Rome. Originally known as the Flavian amphitheatre, the Colosseum is impressive even in ruins.

As you stand and stare you can imagine the place thronging with crowds. It was started by Emperor Vespasian, built on the site of an artificial lake and part of Nero's huge park in the very centre of Rome. Vespasian's son Titus put the finishing touches to it in 80 AD.

If you thought modern day football arenas were big, that's nothing! The Colosseum is colossal! The elliptical building is about 48.5 m (160 ft) high and in its heyday 55,000 spectators could fit in through an amazing 80 entrances.

Evidence of Roman hierarchy is all around. The place has four storeys, the top tier was for lower classes and women. The lowest level was saved for the rich folk. And under the ground there were cages containing wild animals that could be raised up and released into the arena for entertainment.

The Romans used the Colosseum to show off and put on shows for people, to emphasise their power. The games were free which helped to increase the reigning Emperor's popularity! The events would include displays of exotic animals and fights to the death between animals and gladiators or between two gladiators.

The fact that it is now in ruins isn't just due to natural wear and tear. The southern side was destroyed by an earthquake and parts of the façade were used for other buildings.

STONEHENGE

WILTSHIRE, UK

Steeped in history, mythology and spirituality, Stonehenge is seen as a centre of great importance to many, particularly the druids. Legends around the stones are boundless. It is associated with Arthurian legend, it is said that Merlin arranged the removal of the stones from Ireland where they had been hewn by giants.

The true meaning of Stonehenge is lost in the mists of time. It could have been a temple for worshipping the sun, a burial site or a calendar to mark important astrological events. The mystery and uncertainty of its origins make it all the more attractive.

They may just look like a pile of stones, but the dedication and determination of those who positioned them as far back as 300 BC, is awe-inspiring. Workers would have only had basic tools like antler picks, yet they managed to dig a deep enclosing ditch and build a huge bank around the area where the stones sit.

Stonehenge's position in relation to the rising and setting of the sun is legendary and no one knows whether this was because they were sun worshippers or merely needed a calendar to work out the days and months of the year.

As you get closer and closer to the stones, their size and the sheer human effort of getting them in position becomes apparent. Building a patio wall will never seem so difficult ever again!

101
189

lost in the MIST of time

home  to

fabulous

FRESCOES

POMPEII RUINS
CAMPANIA, ITALY

Pompeii was an ordinary little town like any other until the day in 79 AD when Mount Vesuvius erupted, burying buildings and its 20,00 inhabitants in deadly ash, pumice and soil. Everyone was killed and it wasn't until thousands of years later that archaeologists began to uncover the site.

Now a UNESCO World Heritage Site, the town is one of the most visited places in Italy. Lengthy excavations over many years have discovered a treasure trove of well-preserved buildings, including the Forum, Thermal Baths and several villas.

Many everyday items were found and these finds give an intimate picture of what life would have been like in the first century AD. The people of this prosperous little port were completely unaware that Mount Vesuvius was a volcano as it hadn't erupted for 1,800 years.

When archaeologists began to uncover the town they even found bread in the ovens that had been baking on the day. If you're feeling a little ghoulish, there are plaster casts of people who would have been killed on the day.

Pompeii is an easy trip from Rome or Naples. Take your time to check out the place with its thermal baths, a brothel and Vetti's House which is home to fabulous frescoes. If you're visiting in the summer, avoid the middle of the day when it's hottest, which is also the time many cruise ships stop by, so it's busier then.

PARTHENON
ATHENS, GREECE

The Parthenon is dedicated to the goddess Athena. The people of Athens believed her to be their patron. It is situated on top of the Greek Acropolis, the highest hill in the city. The building has been on the site for years, but it was destroyed by the Persians around 480 BC.

For years the site was left in ruins until architects Callicrates and Icticus, along with sculptor Pheidias were brought in. Their aim was to make it the best temple ever and their determination is visible.

When you look around you'll find lots of touches to out-do the designs of other temples, a real example of architectural one-upmanship. For example, temples usually have six columns across the front, but the Parthenon has eight. It also has both Doric and ionic columns, whereas it's usually one or the other.

The place is a wondrous architectural treasure. Among the highlights is a frieze that runs round the exterior walls of the building. It was partially destroyed in 1687 as the Ottoman Turks used the building as a gunpowder store and after being hit by a Venetian mortar, a huge part of it was left in ruins.

Over half the artefacts are in the Acropolis Museum in Athens, except for the Elgin Marbles, which were brought to Britain by the Earl of Elgin in the early 1800s. They rest in the British Museum and are at the centre of a dispute as the Greeks want them back.

THE PYRAMIDS
EGYPT

A visit to the tombs of the pharaohs is high on everyone's list, not least because of the mind-numbing scale of the construction involved. The Egyptians believed that if a pharaoh's body was mummified after death, he would be able to live forever.

These massive tombs were designed to protect the buried pharaoh's body and his belongings. When you arrive you will simply be overwhelmed by the size of the pyramids. The biggest, the Great Pyramid, is the largest.

At over 140 m (459 ft) tall, it took 20 years to construct and was made for the Pharaoh Khuf. Even though the Pyramids offer what must look like a water-tight method of burial, the Egyptians still believed extra protection was needed.

So, to guard their pharaohs further, they built the Sphinx. With the body of a lion and the head of a pharaoh, it stood as a seriously impressive guard in front of the pyramids in Giza.

A trip to the Pyramids is a must and as long as you aren't claustrophobic, so is going inside. It opens the door to a whole new world.

Any trip to the pyramids these days is best carefully planned. A lot of commercialism has grown up around the sites but it is still possible to be totally immersed in the mystical grandeur of these beautiful structures.

TERRACOTTA ARMY
XIAN, CHINA

The Terracotta Army was discovered by accident. In 1974, local farmers were digging a well in Xian, China when they broke into a pit that turned out to contain 600 life-size terracotta figures. Further investigations found that there were two more pits filled with terracotta warriors and more underground areas containing the bones of horses and smaller figures.

Terracotta horses and chariots were also unearthed. When excavations finished, almost 8,000 terracotta figures had been recovered. Research shows that the army of statues was guarding the tomb of the Qin Shi Huang di, the First Emperor of China, who lived 2,200 years ago.

He was a massively respected figure, famous for unifying warring states into what we know now as China. It is believed that the terracotta men were made to protect him on his journey to the afterlife.

Each warrior is unique, right down to his clothes and facial expressions. They are all made from clay that dried to the rich red colour terracotta is famous for. The Museum of Qin Terracotta Warriors and Horses houses many of the statues and is laid out in the way it was first discovered, with soldiers at the front and chariots at the back.

As you wander round, it becomes apparent just how long the creation of these men must have taken. The very scale of the Emperor's army will take your breath away.

DISCOVERED

BY

ACCIDENT

SURROUNDED

BY MAGICAL

forests

TIKAL NATIONAL PARK
PETÉN BASIN, GUATEMALA

This national park in the north of Guatemala, is home to some fascinating examples of the ancient Mayan Civilisation. It was worked on by experts from the US Pennsylvania University in 1956 and is the largest excavated site on the American continent.

It took them 13 years to uncover the buildings and even now there are more to find. Tikal is an absolutely breathtaking experience, an ancient city surrounded by magical forests.

Tikal stayed hidden for centuries after the Mayan people suddenly abandoned it over 1,000 years ago. It became overgrown in forests until gum collector Ambrosio Tut saw the very tips of the temples in the distance. Rather than investigate alone, he went back and told the Governor Modesto Mendez. They took an artist with them to record what they found and their findings were published in 1853.

Tikal is an entire city and at its peak, would have been home to an estimated 80,000 people. It features over 3,000 structures including palaces, temples, plazas, ball courts and homes, all set on a grid of streets and terraces.

Even after years of research and excavations, it's still unclear why the city was abandoned. You can come to your own conclusions as you wander round. Tikal is easy to get to and there are plenty of tours available with experienced guides. The area is a cornucopia of fantastic flora and fauna too.

You can't really see everything in a day and if you want to linger longer, there are hotels in the park. If you don't want to see it on foot, there are also helicopter tours that give you a bird's eye view!

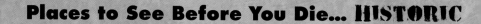

BALMORAL CASTLE
ABERDEENSHIRE, UK

The holiday home of the Royal Family for many years, the brilliant castle of Balmoral is set in awe-inspiring scenery of Royal Deeside, overshadowed by the mountain of Lochnagar. Queen Victoria bought the estate back in 1848 and it has been the Scottish home of the British Royal Family ever since.

Queen Victoria described Balmoral as 'my dear, dear paradise in the Highlands' and if you make the worthwhile journey, you'll probably end up feeling the same. You have nine months of the year to visit, Balmoral is closed to visitors during August, September and October when the Royal Family is in residence.

After Queen Victoria bought the place, it was considered too small for the needs of the Royals and Prince Albert supervised the design of a new building. Apparently, Queen Victoria and Prince Albert bought the building without ever seeing it.

Effectively the whole place was rebuilt and completed and then the old one was demolished. A commemoration stone marks the spot of the front door of the old castle. Even back then, they were very concerned that the castle should be in keeping with its surroundings and the new castle was built with granite from local quarries.

Balmoral offers that little bit extra insight into why the Royals decided to find themselves a bolthole so far north. The estate is also home to many activities, including fishing, activity weekends, guided walks and for the energetic there is even a Balmoral half marathon!

paradise

in the

HIGHLANDS

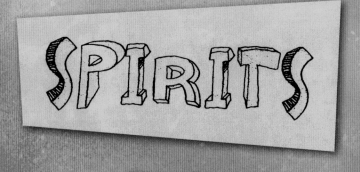

EASTER ISLAND

CHILE, SOUTH AMERICA

One of the most recognisable, but least visited, archaeological sites in the world, probably because of its obscure location. You'll have seen pictures of these giant heads everywhere, huge blocks of dark stone on hillsides staring out over the ocean.

It gets its westernised name from the Dutch sea captain Jacob Roggeveen, who became the first European to visit the island on Easter Sunday, back in 1722.

No one's quite sure who the original inhabitants of the island were, but most theories are that they came from Polynesia and landed on the island's north side. The Moai Statues of Rapi Nui are what make the place famous.

There are around 250 of these massive statues, circling the island like guards. They are believed to represent the spirits of ancestors and great chiefs. Most of them are carved from the stone of the Rano Raraku volcano on the island. They are seriously impressive, averaging around 4.2 m (14 ft) tall.

The most famous site on Easter Island is Ahu Akivi where seven Moais stand with their backs to the sea and the caves of Ana Tepahu. As the place is a long way off, you'll probably want to combine your trip to Easter Island with visiting other places in the area.

Head for the bright lights and easy living of Chile's capital city Santiago, or aim for the hills and discover where Chilean wine comes from!

PETRA RUINS

PETRA, JORDAN

The world of Petra is hidden behind a barrier of imposing mountains, entered through a narrow gorge. It's one of those moments that literally will take your breath away as the dark of the gorge gives way to a natural square of amazing monuments.

Petra is a legacy of the Nabataeans, a hard-working Arab people who settled in Jordan over 2,000 years ago. They planned their home with a thoroughness and attention to detail that seems incredible today. Petra includes some amazing architecture and a complex of dams and water channels.

It is now a UNESCO World Heritage Site. Its most famous monument is The Treasury, El-Khasneh, which dominates the town with its delicate carvings. Petra has over 800 individual monuments: tombs, baths, funeral halls, temples and rows of streets with beautiful colonnades. Most of them are carved from rich sandstone.

The sheer size of the city means you will easily spend a day there, strolling from one place to another, on a seemingly endless trail of marvels. Petra flourished for 400 years until it was occupied by the Roman legions of Emperor Trajan in 106 AD. The best times of day to see the sights are early morning and late afternoon when the sun gives the multi-colored stones a bewitching hue.

natural

SQUARE

 amazing

MOMENTS

wild and

BEAUTIFUL

spot

ROBBEN ISLAND
CAPE TOWN, SOUTH AFRICA

For three hundred years, this island off the coast of South Africa, was used as a place of imprisonment and isolation. The most famous person to have languished on the island was Nelson Mandela, who was kept there for many years. Famously he went on to become South Africa's first democratic President.

Nelson Mandela was arrested in 1962 and was convicted of sabotage and sentenced to life in prison. He spent 27 years inside, many of them on the island itself, you can visit his cell and see what life was like as a political prisoner.

Others incarcerated on Robben include Robert Sobukwe, the founding leader of the Pan African Congress. Further back, indigenous African leaders, Muslim leaders from the East Indies, Dutch and British soldiers, women and many anti-apartheid activists have all been holed up in the place.

Inevitably this makes it a sobering place to visit. It has only been a museum and heritage site since 1997, though it wasn't always used as a prison. Because of its isolation, during Victorian times and the first part of the 20th century, it was also used as a hospital for people with leprosy, and the mentally ill. It was chosen as it was secure, there was no way for people to escape and also because the sea air was deemed to help people recover.

To get to the island, you take a half hour ferry ride from the Nelson Mandela Gateway in Cape Town. It's a wild and beautiful spot, home to a over a hundred different bird species. The journey over gives you a chance to look out for some magnificent marine mammals, including Cape Fur seals and Heaviside Dolphins.

TOWER OF LONDON
LONDON, UK

Step back into the murky past of London with a trip to the majestic Tower, home to all kinds of dark deeds and legends. For over 900 years, this magnificent grey building has stood guard over the city. In its time, it has been put to all manner of uses as a palace, Royal mint, arsenal, place of execution, jewel house and even a Royal zoo.

Built by William the Conqueror after his successful invasion in 1066, it is best known for being a prison and that's where all the grisly stories come from. Prisoners would be brought to the Tower by boat.

The executioner would stand behind the accused and crowds would hang around waiting to find out if he was guilty. With the execution taking place two days later! Lots of people were executed at the Tower, including Henry VIII's wives Anne Boleyn and Catherine Howard, and Lady Jane Grey, known as the Nine Day Queen. It's not all gruesome, though as the Crown Jewels are kept here.

Crammed with over 20,000 precious gems, including crowns, orbs, robes and sceptres. You can also admire weaponry and armour used through the ages. Many tours are led by Yeoman Warders, known as Beefeaters, who have plenty of tales to tell.

No visit to the Tower is complete without sight of one of the famous ravens. Legend has it that if these black birds ever leave the Tower, it will crumble and things will go horribly wrong in England!

guard OVER THE CITY

ROMAN BATHS

BATH, UK

The Romans were clean and very sociable people as you'll find out when you step into this marvellously preserved example of public baths from hundreds of years ago. The Roman Baths themselves are below street level.

It's a fascinating trip, especially as you can imagine how it must have been to soak in the water back in Roman times, then talk about it over a cup of tea in the Pump Room, built in the late 1700s! It's amazing to think the place attracted so many people over so many centuries.

The water that bubbles through the Baths came from the Mendip Hills. With its presumed health giving properties, it made for a pleasant way for Romans to pass the time. Later, in Georgian times, it was the norm for well-to-do families to move to Bath, from London, for a few weeks each year to experience the health benefits of fresh air and spa waters.

These days visitors aren't allowed in the water, mainly due to the health risks as it passes through lead pipes. Voted the Most Romantic Building in Britain by the Royal Association of British Architects in 2010, the Roman Baths include four main features: the Sacred Spring, the Roman Temple, the bath house and an exhibition of finds from Roman Bath.

Hot water rises at the Sacred Spring. The Romans didn't realise it was a natural phenomenon and believed it was the work of ancient gods. To ensure the supply was maintained, the Romans built a temple next to the spring, to Sulis Minerva, a goddess with healing powers.

BRANDENBURG GATE

BERLIN, GERMANY

ou can't fail to be inspired by the sheer size of the gate, whose design was based on the Propylaea (the gateway to the Acropolis in Athens). This majestic gateway was commissioned by Friedrick Wilhelm II to symbolise peace when it was first constructed in 1791.

Bearing that in mind, it's quite bizarre that the gate was incorporated into the Berlin Wall during the years that kept the city in two distinct halves. East Berlin was under Communist rule while the West side was part of a democracy.

Nowadays, the gate stands as a symbol of the reunification of the two sides of this great city, but from the construction of the Wall in 1961 until 1989 the Brandenburg Gate was inaccessible to the general public.

You can trace the site of the wall and even look out for metallic animals in the asphalt on Chausee Street, a reminder that for years only rabbits were free to hop back and forth between the two sides of Berlin.

Look out for Checkpoint Charlie, the most popular crossing point between East and West Berlin. This is now a museum telling the story of the wall and the day it came down during peaceful demonstrations in 1989.

something

 a

PILGRIMAGE

BEACHES OF NORMANDY

NORMANDY, FRANCE

A trip to the beaches of Normandy will bring a lump to your throat as you recall the climactic Second World War battle of Dunkirk, D Day. During the night of June 6, 1944, 135,000 men and 20,000 vehicles were brought on to the shores of Normandy using five landing beaches.

Many experienced companies now offer the opportunities to visit the five beaches: Sword, Juno, Gold, Omaha, Pointe du Hoc and soak in some of the sobering atmosphere that surrounds the place.

Visiting the beaches can be seen as something of a pilgrimage. It is best to incorporate some history in to your trip and one of the best places to start is the Caen Memorial in the town of Caen.

As well as a tribute to the people who were killed in the battle for the town, it also has a museum that explains more about the causes of the Second World War and the course it took. Take a breather to reflect in one of three memorial gardens, each one dedicated to the British, American and Canadian allies.

No visit is complete without a visit to at least one of the many war cemeteries in the area. Around 100,000 soldiers died during those battles in the summer of 1944, around 40,000 Allies and 60,000 Germans. Some were repatriated but the vast majority were laid to rest in the peaceful countryside not far from the coast.

There are a numbing 26 different military cemeteries in the area, each one offering a haven of tranquillity and all are maintained with the utmost respect.

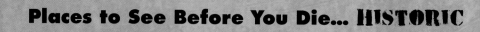

LA SAGRADA FAMÍLIA

BARCELONA, SPAIN

comparative youngster considering the great age of some churches! Construction of the Segrada Família only begun in 1883 and work still isn't quite complete! It is close to the hearts of Spanish catholics as it is known as an expiatory church, one built entirely from the donations of the people.

It was designed by Antoni Gaudi, seen to be one of the key figures of Catalan culture. Building the Segrada Família occupied most of his professional life. Sadly, his talent was cut short when he was knocked down by a tram and died later of his injuries. Aptly, he is buried in the Carmen chapel of the crypt.

As well as being a strikingly beautiful building, Segrada Família has a great sense of place. Wander down the aisles and you will feel part of the massive community that made it possible. Even a small donation as you visit will go to ensuring that the building is eventually finished. Although it is incomplete, it is a UNESCO World Heritage Site and in 2010 it was proclaimed as a minor basilica by Pope Benedict XVI.

It attracts over 2 million visitors a year, making it Barcelona's top attraction and the size and scope of the place is hard to imagine until you're standing inside the building. Make the place an integral part of a trip to the Spanish city. While you are there take in a couple more places that have Gaudi stamped all over them: Casa Batllo is a grand house originally built for a wealthy aristocrat and is now a museum; and Park Guell, a peaceful park of colourful sculptures and mosaics.

strictly

beautiful

BUILDING

THE KREMLIN

MOSCOW, RUSSIA

The top of everyone's list on a trip to Russia and you can see why. Over the centuries, the Kremlin, in the heart of Red Square has been everything from a medieval citadel to a modern powerhouse.

As you walk towards it, you will sense a massive feeling of its might. The Kremlin is absolutely huge and even though two thirds of it are closed to visitors, the rest contains enough fascinating things to see to last you more than one trip!

There have been people living on the site for hundreds of years, but the first actual building was erected in the 1100s when Yuri Dolgoruky, the Grand Duke of Kiev built a fort. The citadel was fortified with stone walls and the city of Moscow grew up around it, forming a private complex.

Ivan the Great's descendents worked on developing the place further and even when Peter the Great moved the Russian capital to St. Petersburg, Moscow still remained an important place. After the Revolution in 1917, the Kremlin got its power back as the seat of Russian government and the official residence of the President.

The Kremlin has palaces, museums and churches. The Armory Palace houses a spectacular collection of Fabergé eggs, wedding clothes and many royal coaches from the days when Russia was ruled by tsars. Also, keep a lookout for the watchtower known as the 'Ivan the Great Bell Tower', which was used to keep a lookout over the city. There are 21 bells inside and it takes a staggering 24 people just to set them in motion.

VALLEY OF THE KINGS
LUXOR, EGYPT

This remote valley is home to the final resting place of some of the best known Pharaohs, notably Tutankhamun and Rameses the Great. Effectively the Valley of the Kings was a royal cemetery. A phenomenal 62 Pharaohs are buried here and it was a place closely guarded by sentries.

The only entrance to the valley was a long winding path. Guards stood at the top of the hills, their aim was to stop tomb raiders. Not surprisingly, robbing loot from the tomb of a dead king was a very lucrative business and well worth the risk to some people.

Each tomb is named KV with a number following it to show when it was discovered. KV 62, the tomb of Tutankhamun, is the most recently unearthed. Egyptologist John Gardiner Wilkinson established the present numbering system in 1827. The earliest known tomb belongs to Tuthmoses I who established the valley as a royal burial site.

Choosing which tomb to visit is a tough choice, but the Tomb of Amonhotep II (KV 35) is said to be one of the best in the valley. It is crammed with religious scenes and was discovered in 1897. It contains the mummies of several kings and queens. If you can brave the queues, the tomb of Tutankhamun is a must. Though he was a relatively minor king, his tomb was found more or less intact and had survived being robbed, as over 3,500 items were discovered buried with him.